£2.00

D0363425

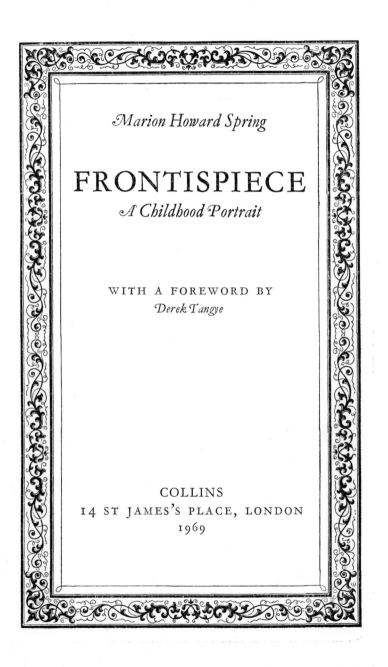

Marion Howard Spring

FRONTISPIECE
A Childhood Portrait

WITH A FOREWORD BY
Derek Tangye

COLLINS
14 ST JAMES'S PLACE, LONDON
1969

For Susan Marion Rose,
with love

Contents

Foreword

BY DEREK TANGYE

I read *Frontispiece* and found myself thinking of Mrs Gaskell's *Cranford*. Marion Howard Spring's book is not a novel, but her detail of incidents long ago, her description of standards which seemed at the time indestructible, her gift of making casual moments come alive, remind me of the serenity of Mrs Gaskell's story.

Marion Spring herself is a serene person. You can call on her at any time at the White Cottage in Falmouth (and people visit her from all over the world) and you feel a happier person as soon as she greets you. I was there the other day and found her, as so many times before, pottering in the greenhouse, watercan in hand, caring for the seedlings, plants and cacti which are so much a part of her life.

Her garden, the garden created by her and Howard Spring, is one of the most colourful in Cornwall. She opens it to the public four times a year for the benefit of charitable causes; and garden-lovers old and young flock there, stand beneath the giant turkey oak which rises from the edge of the lawn, and wander along the paths bordered with rare plants and shrubs. Marion

Spring answers questions, explains whence this plant or that came, but takes little credit for the pleasure she is giving. 'Howard found this plant,' she says. Or: 'Howard designed this border.'

One feels that Howard Spring still lives in the house and walks the garden. Marion Spring has conveyed this mood first in *Memories and Gardens*, then in the biography *Howard*. In both these books she succeeded, by avoiding self-conscious writing, in delighting her readers with the story of their love affair. All forty-five years of it.

But in the present book there is very little mention of Howard Spring until the end. She writes instead about the small things she remembers of her childhood and her youth.

'Mother delighted to dress me in the Kate Greenaway fashion. I can remember a frock of apple-green brocade, reaching almost to the ground, with low neck and short puffed sleeves, and a Dorothy-bag of the same material hanging from the sash.'

'On Monday evenings we all went to dancing-class, and Mrs Bedford, who taught us, was supposed to be the best teacher of ballroom dancing in London. She had an assistant with a wooden leg, called Miss Dagnall, who was also a very good teacher, though she was a bit heavy to waltz with.'

Such incidents one might rightly describe as trivia. But what is wrong with that? Sensation is not the beginning and end of life. And trivia help to place the acclaimed achievements of today in a saner perspective.

I treasure my friendship with Howard and Marion Spring, and I am honoured that she asked me to write the foreword to this charming, tender story.

Introduction

If I could bend my sadness to abide
     In fealty to the gladdening rule of spring;
     If all the richnesses of June should swing
Across my heart, a deep, harmonious tide;
If Autumn all her silvern tenderness
     Should spin about me with like dewy threads
     To those that spiders throw from roses' heads
Athwart a morning lily's slenderness;
If winter's slow and ruminant content,
     In cold and numb Lethean wave on wave,
     Should lap me round and bring me to the grave
Of all my troubled thought's experiment:
     How, even then, could I for long put by
     Dreams of the dead and those who yet must die?
                    HOWARD SPRING: *Haunted*

When I lost my dear husband, Howard Spring, on
May 3rd, 1965, I felt that life would be insupportable
without him. For forty-five years he had been the
perfect companion and the way ahead looked bleak
and barren. The wound has never healed, but gradually
I realize that I must make the best of what remains—
family and friends, cats, garden and memories.

A year after his death I started to write his biography,

and when this was published it brought me letters from all over the world—England, Ireland and Scotland, South Africa, Rhodesia, Malaysia, New Zealand, Australia, East and West Germany, Canada, America and Venezuela, and it was clear that readers of his novels loved him through his books. These letters brought me comfort, and I have answered them all.

I live with my four cats: Perkins, a black satin boy; Penguin, black and white and very sentimental; Gem, tabby and immaculate white; and Gumbo, a large tabby. When I open my bedroom door in the morning there they are waiting for me. They sit on the stairs while I am having my bath and I have to be very careful not to trip over them when I go down to breakfast. They hang about the kitchen while I am working, and as soon as I sit down they jump on my lap, all four of them, purring a harmonious quartet. They are very good company.

My elder son, David, lives only five miles away, so that I see him and his charming wife, Runa, nearly every week-end, and the children, Susan and Robert, too, when they are home on holiday. My younger son, Michael, lives in Dorking, Surrey, and sometimes he comes to stay with me for a few days, and takes me for lovely rides. Cornwall is still a very beautiful county if one avoids caravan sites and other uglinesses. The coastline is superb.

One friend pops in nearly every week-end with a loaf of delicious home-made bread which she has baked for me; another comes and tells me all about the doings of the local Floral Arrangement Society, of which I was once Chairman and am now an honorary lifetime old member; another looks in for a talk about books and the theatre. We have a most delightful little theatre in Falmouth, and I have the honour to be President of the Falmouth Theatre Club.

Then there is the garden and greenhouse. There is always something that must be done. Just now I am taking chrysanthemum cuttings for myself and my friends to give colour and beauty very late in the year, after the dahlias have been cut down by frost. They have to be seen to every day—watering, stopping, feeding, repotting, disbudding, etc. Seed sowing time has come again. This year it looks as if a miracle is about to happen. A visitor from South Africa came to my garden about ten years ago, and when he returned home he sent me some seeds of *Strelitzia Regina*. Three germinated and I tended them with care until they were big plants with handsome leaves, but they had none of the exotic Bird of Paradise flowers. This year a new strange sheathed stem has shot up and I am keeping my fingers crossed because I believe there is a flower-bud on the end of it.

Many years ago Howard gave me a Clivia, and it

had deep yellow trumpet flowers every year. Then it left off blooming. The books tell one that it flowers best if it is pot-bound, but evidently mine was too pot-bound. So last autumn I prised it out of its pot, soaked it in the tank, then carefully divided the root until I had ten separate pieces all with large leathery strap-shaped leaves. I potted them up and now in January buds have already appeared on three of the plants. Garden and greenhouse are full of surprises and disappointments; something new seems to happen every day. It is never boring.

I get no comfort from the newspapers: war, trade union disputes, labour troubles, student demonstrations, drugs, the Pill, the permissive age, wage snatches by criminals, all disheartening and horrifying. Where are the fine descriptive articles which were such a joy to read? One thing, however, stands like a rock, and that is the crossword puzzle. Nothing nasty here, but a good exercise of the mind. I remember when Howard and I came across the first one in the *Daily Mail* when we were at Llanfairfechan playing with our little boys on the sand. It was a very easy crossword, four-letter words, but not nasty ones. I now always do the *Daily Telegraph* crossword while I am having my lonely lunch, and it seems to get more and more difficult, and more and more interesting. I am very seldom defeated.

And so time passes quickly with all the routine jobs, —cooking, washing up, gardening, brushing the cats, replenishing the bird-table, letter-writing. Emerson says: 'To fill the hour—that is Happiness.' Well, if not happiness, it at least prevents one from being a misery to oneself and everybody else. When I am too tired to do any more chores I sit down in my chair, the cats climb on my lap and memory comes into play. They are lovely memories, a rising tide of happiness, with occasional plunges into the depths of misery and occasional soaring up to the heights of ecstasy.

Many of my correspondents have asked me to write another book: 'Now you have put your hand to the plough, please do not turn back;' 'Please tell us more about your life;' 'I should like to hear more about the cats, I cannot resist a cat book.' And so I am going to try to write about my life from the beginning, as a little girl in a happy middle-class late-Victorian family.

CHAPTER ONE

Baby

All night long and every night,
When my mamma puts out the light
I see the people marching by,
As plain as day, before my eye.

Armies and emperors and kings,
All carrying different kinds of things,
And marching in so grand a way,
You never saw the like by day.

ROBERT LOUIS STEVENSON

I came upon the scene on April 29th, 1890, in a house
in West End Lane, Hampstead. I don't remember
much about that house, because we left it when I was
three years old. Memory is a strange thing. I think we
remember remembering all through our lives, like
two facing mirrors. The reflection gets smaller and
smaller and more and more distant, but always clear.
The first thing that comes to mind is when I was left
alone in the nursery. There was a large coal fire with a
high fender round it, and on the fender little garments
were put to air. The flickering flames reflected those
garments on the nursery wall until they seemed to

have a life of their own. It grew dark and I was very glad when Old Annie came in with a lamp, and the little people on the wall disappeared. Then I was aware once of being in my pram when a man leaned over it in a gorgeous smoking-cap with a bright tassel, and he said: 'Goodbye, Baby.' I expect he was a lodger, for the house was too big for us, but my mother, being a singer, had to keep up appearances.

On their marriage certificate my father was described as a warehouseman, but he must have been a very ambitious and hard-working man, for as soon as I knew anything about him he was a partner in the firm of George Pratt and Co., cotton merchants of London. George Pratt was not so much a sleeping partner as a sailing partner. He had a lovely yacht, called *Lurline*, which he kept at Burnham-on-Crouch, and I don't think the office saw very much of him. Certainly, I never met him. He was a great expert at making sloe gin, and when the brew was ready he would put an advertisement in *The Times*, summoning his cronies to a party. There is a lot to be said for sloe gin as a liqueur. I have made many a bottle of it myself, as sloes grow plentifully on Cornish hedges. Father worked with another ambitious warehouseman. He kept telling Father that he would love to be an actor. Father told him there was no future in it and advised him to stick to cotton. However, this would-be actor left George Pratt and Co., and the next thing Father heard of him was as the famous actor, Edward Compton. Later on a dear little girl was sometimes brought to the warehouse by her father to play hide-and-seek among the cotton bales. This was Fay Compton.

Father's hair turned snow-white when he was in his early twenties, so that he never seemed to grow old. A miniature I have of him when he was nearly seventy years old might have been painted when he was thirty.

My mother had a lovely soprano voice, which was trained by an Italian master. She was born in Swansea and, being very pretty, she was known as the Rose of Swansea. She had very long brown hair and blue eyes. Before her marriage she used to go on concert tours all over England and Scotland. She then used her own maiden name, Miss Ellen Lamb, and on these concert tours she generally went with a contralto, a tenor and a bass. One of the men was called Santley and the contralto was Miss Ira Aldridge, daughter of the then famous American Negro actor, also called Ira Aldridge. I cannot remember the name of the other member of the quartet. After her marriage, Mother still used the name by which she was well known, but then it was *Madame* Ellen Lamb. I think she and Father met when they were in the choir of Rosslyn Hill Unitarian Chapel in Hampstead. Two years after they were married twin boys arrived, and this put an end to Mother's long tours. But she still sang in the choir, gave singing lessons and sang at concerts and public dinners.

I was born five years after the twins, and having coped with them she found me no trouble at all. Sometimes when she went to teach wealthy young ladies to warble their songs in the drawing-room after dinner she was asked to take me with her. I would be put to kick on a rug in front of the fire while I listened to scales and arpeggios and ballads, and when the lesson was finished they would pick me up and play with me.

Mother was very clever with her needle and made all her own clothes, including her hats. She made herself a fetching little bonnet of grey velvet trimmed with pink roses, and one of the Rothschild young women was terribly smitten with it and asked if Mother could make her another like it.

When Mother brought the bonnet, Miss Rothschild asked how much it had cost.

'Five shillings,' said Mother.

'Good gracious, only five guineas!' said Miss Rothschild. 'It's the cheapest bonnet I've ever had, and the prettiest.'

I used to love to sit on Mother's lap and hear all about her adventures as a singer. Mother was not much of a cuddler, she was always too busy with one thing or another, but I would say: 'Now, Mother, please don't kiss me and push me away! I want to hear all about your adventures.' So Mother would tell me how, after a successful concert in Edinburgh, some men in the enthusiastic audience took the horses out of her carriage and took her to her hotel by manpower; and how she went to stay with Madame Adelina Patti in a castle in Wales. A macabre thing she told me was that once when she was staying in lodgings, she hung up in the wardrobe her evening dress, which was of pink taffeta with little roses all round the neckline. When she came to put it on she found black beetles nestling in the roses!

Mother kept a press-cutting book, but alas! this was burnt by my stepmother. So, too, was the Victorian photograph album, with portraits going back to the beginnings of photography. I used to love looking at this album. It was the kind which used to lie on a crochet mat on a table at an angle to the family Bible. The pictures were slid in between double pages, and the openings were ornamented with a border of flowers, pansies, roses, maidenhair fern, etc. I remember a photograph of my father which must have been taken over a hundred years ago. He looked a dear cherub about three years old dressed in a low-necked dark silk frock, with little buttons all down the front. When he was a small boy spelling bees were all the rage—difficult words were given out round the ring of competitors and anyone who made a mistake was eliminated. Father always emerged triumphant. This passion for words was handed down in the family: the boys and I did not have to learn to read, we just read. I was started on *Rosebud*, then on to *Playbox*, then *Chatterbox*. After that the whole world of books was open to me. I still love words—magical words in which everything beautiful has been written—and at my elbow I keep *Webster's Collegiate Dictionary*, which not only gives the clear meaning of any word I have not come across before, but also beautiful line drawings of birds, animals, fishes, flowers, architecture, classical figures, tools and almost everything that can be illustrated.

When I was three years old we left our large house in Hampstead and went to live in a little one in Harlesden. At that time, in 1893, it was almost a village. I recently heard from an old lady who lives there and she says that it is now all changed. Stonebridge Park, where there were large residences with beautiful gardens, is full of eighteen-storey blocks of council flats, labour offices, welfare offices. In fact, she tells me that the whole neighbourhood is full of high blocks of flats and gone are the gardens. I should not like to go back there.

But seventy-five years ago it was a pleasant enough

suburb, and the front gardens had hawthorn-trees, laburnum and cherry trees hanging over the roads, so that the place had a pastoral air. No. 5 Stracey Road, where we went to live, was a small semi-detached house with a little front garden, a long side passage leading to the kitchen door, where in time the twins and I used to play soft-ball cricket with the wicket marked in chalk on the back of the entrance door, and the usual oblong of garden at the back. There was a dining-room, drawing-room, kitchen and scullery on the ground floor and a passage leading to the End Room which was the boys' playroom. There were four bedrooms and a dressing-room on the first floor and a roomy landing, which I had as my playroom. I was rather afraid of the End Room, for the boys kept white mice there, which smelt revolting, and also they in time started experiments with electricity, and it was of course their delight to give me frightful shocks. But this was much later.

As well as making some of her own clothes, Mother made all mine. She delighted to dress me in the Kate Greenaway fashion. I can remember a frock of apple-green brocade, reaching almost to the ground, with low neck and short puffed sleeves, and a Dorothy-bag of the same material hanging from the sash. Then there was another dress I remember of white delaine with pink roses on it, a pink sash, pink ribbon tie-ups on my shoulders and, of course, the usual Dorothy-bag for my hankie.

She made me a caped coat and bonnet of white face-cloth trimmed with grebe, and I can remember standing on a sheet with my eyes closed while Mother and Old Annie sprinkled glitter over me to go to a fancy-dress party at the Vicarage in Stonebridge Park. I had a robin on my bonnet, another on my shoulder and another on my grebe-trimmed muff, and I was supposed to represent Winter. A very minute Winter! When I was ready to go Annie surveyed me with her head on one side, and said: 'You'll do, with a bit of butter!' which was the highest praise that I ever got from her.

On another occasion when I went to a summer fancy-dress party, Mother made me a white dress which I wore with a wreath of white Bennett's Seedling roses, while my doll was dressed in her silk frock trimmed with crimson rambler roses. Her mailcart which I pushed was painted white and decked with striped red and white roses, Gloria Mundi. We were supposed to represent the Wars of the Roses. The striped rose was prolific in our little garden, but now when I try to grow it in Cornwall it does all right for a year, then next year has all red roses on it.

For a few years after we went to live in Harlesden, Father and Mother continued to sing in the choir at Rosslyn Hill Unitarian Chapel, and they always took me with them on Sunday mornings. It was there that I was christened by Dr Brook Herford with water from the River Jordan which he had brought home in a bottle. Some of the ladies in the congregation made quite a pet of me. One Christmas morning Mother brought a small red leather trunk and put it on my cot. When I opened it I found a most beautiful doll inside and a complete wardrobe of clothes, all exquisitely hand-made—a pink silk frock, brown velvet coat and bonnet, underclothes trimmed with tiny hand-made lace, nightdress, dressing-gown, shoes and stockings. If those ladies of Rosslyn Hill could have known what pleasure that lovely present gave me for years and years, I think they would have been repaid for all the trouble they had taken. I had very long fine brown hair, and I used to grizzle every day when it was brushed and combed. So Mother had it cut short, and when my doll lost her hair through over-much attention, Mother had my own hair made into a wig for her which I could brush and comb and plait to my heart's content.

Mother was away from home so often, singing and giving lessons, that I was largely left in the care of Old Annie. She had been maid to my grandmother, and when she died Annie came to live with us. She was a devout Wesleyan and belonged to their local literary and debating societies. If we missed our dictionary we could generally find it in the kitchen. She was very careful about my speech, and one day I blotted my copy-book very badly. The Wesleyan minister had come to pay her a visit and I ran up to him and said: 'Look! I was just mucking about with a piece of linen and silk and needle and I found I was doing real featherstitch!' 'MISS MARION! Where did you learn such language!' Then, turning apologetically to her visitor: 'I suppose it's those boys.' I loved her dearly, and I think she was very fond of me. She taught me long poems, which I used to recite to my parents with great pride—'Casabianca', 'The Leak in the Dyke', 'The Fireman's Wedding', and so on. Father and Mother must have been tired of hearing them, but they were very polite.

Just round the corner from Stracey Road, along Knatchbull Road into Craven Park Road, there was Miss Biddlecombe's School of Deportment, and when I was four years old I attended her classes twice a week. I cannot remember very much about it, except that we had to march round the room with wooden rings on our heads and do 'action' songs. When I was five I went to Miss Search's kindergarten where we learnt to do all sorts of things with coloured papers and prickers and blocks. I suppose it was good training for manual dexterity, which I have had all my life. While I was there I had my first plunge into the depths of misery.

I had been reading about a little girl who was cruelly treated at school. So, wishing to dramatize myself, I told Mother that I had been made to stand on a form for a long time with a book balanced on my head. It was an absolute lie, for dear Miss Search would not have been in the least bit unkind. However, Mother took me firmly by the hand and marched me to school. My heart sank lower and lower into my boots. It felt like lead, and when I got to the Constitutional Hall, which was just opposite to the kindergarten, I burst out crying and confessed. I think Mother saw by my woebegone face that I had been sufficiently punished, for she said no more about it. When I got home Old Annie had heard about it, for she said: 'Let it be a lesson to you!' And it certainly was.

My bedroom was opposite to Annie's, at the end of a long passage, and our windows looked out on the back garden. When I had been tucked into bed, Mother or Annie heard me say my prayers:

> Gentle Jesus, meek and mild,
> Look upon a little child.
> Pity my simplicity;
> Suffer me to come to Thee.

Then the Lord's Prayer, and then God's blessing on Father and Mother, Algy and Reggie, Annie, aunties and uncles and cousins, Mary White (my Rosslyn Hill doll), Tibber (my cat) and Conrad Tattersall Pye (our collie dog), after which they would kiss me good-night and close the door.

Then strange things would begin to happen. Generally, the light had not yet gone out of the sky, and as I looked at the plain wall of my bedroom strange kaleidoscopic shapes would appear. Then sometimes I would see a procession of men and horses moving along the wall. When later I went to the Haberdashers' Aske's Girls' School in Acton, and saw the copy of the Parthenon frieze round the Big Hall, I recognized my men and horses. Was I trailing some clouds of Grecian glory into my little girlhood? I never spoke about these visions but I found them somewhat comforting and reassuring. Sir Osbert Sitwell in his autobiography talks about a grey shape that went across his bedroom wall, but that was understandable at ancient Renishaw. My phantoms came to a small semi-detached new suburban house, with no history. I wonder if other little girls have had a similar experience?

In the 1890's, to compensate for our hard winters we had the most beautiful summers. The skies hardly ever seemed to be clouded, and if we had rain on three days running it was a phenomenon to be wondered at. The lawn would go brown and cracks would appear, and I would watch the ants climbing out of the cracks and going busily about their work, sometimes carrying

ants' eggs. The garden was my joy then, as gardens
have been ever since. It was the usual long rectangle,
lawn in the middle with standard roses in small beds
all round, then the path with border beyond. The roses
were grown to perfection. Black spot and other
diseases did not seem to exist in those days. The
standards were sprayed with a solution of quassia chips
plus a little soft soap and a drop or two of paraffin.
This kept the greenfly at bay. They were fed with a
solution of soot and manure, which was put in a
chequered cotton bag and suspended in the rain-water
barrel.

I was given a book about Queen Victoria and I read
that when she was a child living in Kensington Palace
she had a garden of her very own, and how she used
to water her own feet as much as the garden. So I
promised Mother that if she would give me a bit of
ground, I would not water my feet. She made me a
kind of rockery with bits of clinker near the kitchen
door where Annie could keep an eye on me. It did not
get much sunshine, but I managed to grow London
pride, rather lanky Virginia stock, ferns and fuchsias,
and never a weed did I let grow there.

Gradually I was allowed to look after the violas that
grew round the rose-beds, and they were lovely, with
long crisp stems that you could snap off where they
joined the leaves. Mr Morbey, the head gardener of

Roundwood Park, used to give us some of his time in the evenings, and he would give me some viola cuttings—Archie Grant, Maggie Mott, Duchess of Fife, White Queen and Blue Prince. I suppose our garden was so small that each plant could have individual attention, and they certainly paid for it. I have never seen better roses or violas.

After a while Father and Mother found it too tiring to go to Rosslyn Hill Chapel every Sunday morning after a hard week's work, so we all went to the church of St Michael and All Angels, which was just at the bottom of the garden. Father and Reg were in the choir and Mother, Algy and I had our own seats in the church. To start with, I went to the morning service and the afternoon children's service, but soon I went to the evening service as well, and enjoyed it all very much. But a man in the choir wrote to the Bishop and complained that we were a family of Unitarians. Father and Reg were asked to leave the choir, though the Vicar was very reluctant to do so, especially as Father was a guarantor for quite a large amount for the Chancel Fund. Thus our church-going came to an end, which was a great pity. At the time when this happened I was being prepared for confirmation, but I found that I could not go on with it.

As I have said, when I was very young we had very hard winters and beautiful summers. I can remember when everybody's pipes were frozen and stand-pipes were put up at intervals along the roads and all water had to be fetched from them. One day Reg, who was pretty tough as a rule, fainted in the choir because of the intense cold and had to be brought home. But fuel was cheap—Best Derby Brights just over a pound a ton—and we always had glorious great fires in the grates. In the summer continuous sunshine was taken for granted. The shops looked very gay with their striped awnings to keep their wares from being faded. A horse in a straw bonnet would draw the watering-cart to keep the dust on the roads down, and the smell of the water on the dust was delightful. The traffic was very varied—butchers' carts drawn by spanking swift horses, brewers' drays drawn by shire horses with their polished brasses, victorias with ladies in their pretty dresses with ruffled sunshades, dashing couples in hansom cabs, the smart turn-outs of doctors, etc., so much more beautiful and interesting than motor-cars.

As one stood with one's back to the house, there was a brick wall as the right-hand boundary, terminating in the brick end of the hothouse next door. On this wall our collie, Conrad Tattersall Pye, used to love to lie and sun himself, and against the hothouse was a lovely white Bennett's Seedling rose. At the end of the garden was a fence with a trellis on top dividing us from the churchyard. It was covered with a beautiful

William Allen Richardson rose and a Paul's Scarlet climber. Under this wall were garden frames, which Father for some reason glazed himself. He certainly was not given to swearing, but he was not very handy, and as the work proceeded the air was filled with 'D-hush! D-hush! D-hush!' The boundary on the left-hand side was a wooden fence with cross-bars. All through the summer this garden was my playground. I would beg a couple of kitchen chairs and an old rug from Annie, build myself a house and take Mary White and Tibber round the garden in an old pram—'taking the family for a ride in the park'. I'm afraid I used to dress Tibber up in a baby's bonnet and cape when I put him in the pram, but he did not seem to mind as we were great friends. Sometimes if Old Annie were in a particularly good mood she would give me a basin of hot water and some soap, put me up a low clothes-line between the branches of rose-trees and I would wash Mary White's handkerchiefs and underclothes. I had a small flat-iron—larger than Mrs Ewing's *Flat Iron for a Farthing*, but not too heavy for me to use. Annie would heat it on the hob in the kitchen, stand me on a stores box so that I could reach the table, spread out the ironing blanket, teach me how to damp down the dry clothes brought in from the sunshine and then I would iron them.

Beyond the brick wall was a charming little garden

owned by a lady painter of the Alma Tadema school. But beyond the fence side lived four boys, Eric, Ernest, Howard and Vernon, and you could hardly call their patch a garden at all. It was a football ground or a cricket pitch, according to the season. One day Mother told me that I must not have anything to do with the boys next door. I did not know it, but one of them had measles. As I emerged from my 'house', Eric climbed up the bars of the fence and asked me if I would like a bite of his apple. It was a very hot day, he tempted me and I fell. Annie was looking out of the window and she rushed out.

'You naughty girl! Just you wait till your mother comes home. Straight up to your room till she comes.' When she did come home I got the only spanking I think I ever had, but that was not the worst of it. We all got measles, one after the other, and we were away from school for a long time. I was very bad and nearly went blind and had to stay in a dark room. I can remember the first time I was allowed to sit up in a chair, wrapped in a blanket, with a little ray of light in the room and a glass of port wine at my elbow. I was getting better.

When we were convalescent we used to roam about the countryside, and one day when we were catching tiddlers in the Brent a stern school inspector came and asked what we were doing out of school and took our names and addresses. We told him we had had measles and heard no more about it. But why wasn't he inspecting schools? Had he taken a day off to catch tiddlers?

Until I was seven years old, I was always called Baby. I suppose it was because the twins were five years older than I was. I was coming back from a walk with the boys one day when Algy said: 'I think it's high time that we left off calling her Baby. She's seven years old, and from now on we'll call her by her proper name—Marion.' I have never forgotten how proud I felt—all of a sudden I had achieved a new status. I was a little girl with a proper name.

CHAPTER TWO

Baby No More

How do you like to go up in a swing,
　Up in the air so blue?
Oh, I do think it the pleasantest thing
　Ever a child can do!
Up in the air and over the wall,
　Till I can see so wide,
River and trees and cattle and all
　Over the countryside—
Till I look down on the garden green,
　Down on the roof so brown—
Up in the air I go flying again,
　Up in the air and down!

ROBERT LOUIS STEVENSON

Now that I was called Marion, my status was altered
considerably. No more Kate Greenaway clothes. No
more pet names. I soon became a real tomboy, and
Mother dressed me accordingly. I wore a Liberty
bodice with black stockings and little white knickers
attached, and over that a blue serge bodice and knickers
with elastic at the knees, all in one piece. Over that a
blue serge skirt. It was a fine outfit for climbing trees.
On Sunday the bodice, knickers and skirt were of
white serge.

Of course I had pretty dresses as well for special occasions. Mother made all my clothes in spite of being such a very busy woman. Apart from her profession, she was a splendid cook, a first-rate needlewoman and a fine housewife. Annie was devoted to her, and so were her successors. There never seemed to be any friction.

Until I was seven or eight I had gone each year to a wonderful garden-party given by two maiden ladies at Rosslyn Hill Chapel at Squires Mount in Hampstead. It seemed to me then a very large and beautiful place, with summer-houses, stone steps and balustrades right out of a Marcus Stone picture. Rumour said that Miss Ellen Terry had called on the ladies and asked if she might see the interior of the house, as she had heard it was very beautiful and she wished to have it reproduced on the stage. The request was refused with frigid courtesy. Actresses were not quite the thing. Neither, it appears, were children when they passed the little cherub stage, for no more invitations came. But those parties were a great joy and I have remembered them all my life. There was no noise and we did not play games. We had tea and wandered from summer-house to summer-house and played with the toys we found there. I still have the present which I was given at the last party seventy years ago—a leather-bound copy of *Feats on the Fiord*, by Harriet Martineau, illustrated by Arthur Rackham.

I left Miss Search's kindergarten and went to a school kept by the Misses Winhall in Nicoll Road, Harlesden. There we were given a good basic education, learning mostly by rote. My reports generally said: 'Always dreaming'. Be that as it may, Miss Trissie was a bit weak on mathematics and when she came on a problem —X equals?—she gave it to me to take home before the lesson so that I could dream over it to some purpose. Problems were jam to me, and Miss Trissie was never let down.

My twin brothers, Algy and Reginald, went to Harlesden College, and there they had the same kind of basic education. Reg was a great hand at maths. Mr Robert McKee, the headmaster, would give his class enough sums to keep them busy the whole afternoon and said they could go home when they had finished them. Reg would arrive home in about a half-hour or less, all his work finished and correct. Later on in life he found his right niche, as he became a chartered accountant, though I suppose there is a great deal more to that than being a mathematical star.

Nowadays people like to sneer at the Victorians as being stuffy. Anything less stuffy than the lives we children led I cannot imagine. We had cold baths every morning, slept with our windows wide open, went for long walks every week-end and felt as free as air. There was not that sense of impending doom that we feel nowadays. If by being stuffy people mean that we did not use dirty words or discuss dirty subjects or behave in what is called a 'permissive' way, then they were quite right. I remember when I was working in the *Manchester Guardian* office at the age of twenty-four I made a typing slip and said 'Damn!' It was just an explosive expression of annoyance with myself. Then I said to Harold Dore, the Parliamentary correspondent, who was in the same room: 'I have heard that there are even worse words than "Damn!" What are they?' He was a marvellous man with words and we had had many discussions about them. He thought for a moment, then said: 'Well, Miss Pye, there are some very nasty words, mostly connected with sex. I don't think there is any need for you to hear them, and I am quite certain that you will never want to use them.'

Apart from our little garden where I spent so much time during our long sunny summers, Father rented a little field, large enough for a tennis court. My great joy there was a big tree, with a swing hung on a large firm branch and steps going round the trunk leading to a platform among the leaves. I used to swing until I felt a bit dizzy, then I would climb into the tree and keep as still as I could and the birds would come quite close to me. If dreaming was my besetting sin, then this was a lovely place to dream. Sometimes a little friend from across the road would come and play with me, but I was quite happy to be alone and I usually had our collie, Conrad, with me. I would march him round the place and teach him to go to heel, to lie down and to give me his paw. When lessons were over he would relax and jump up at me, wagging his tail with joy, nearly knocking me over. He could never manage to climb into the tree, but I think he would have liked to do so.

In a book called *Children and Gardens* written by that wonderful gardener and most versatile of women, Gertrude Jekyll, published by Country Life in 1908, she recommends that children should have 'that greatest of delights', a real little house where they could cook and receive their friends. She must have been writing for very wealthy people, for the little house she describes has a kitchen with a cooking-stove and a sitting-room with a fire so that it could be used in winter, a covered-in porch and every kind of amenity. In fact, just what would nowadays be paradise for a newly-married couple. I saw just such a play-house at Osborne in the Isle of Wight, where Queen Victoria's children learned the rudiments of housekeeping.

Gertrude Jekyll says: 'There are thousands of little girls in England, and small boys too, who would not only delight in working the play-house, but who would in after years visit it again with delight and look back on its lessons of play-work with thankfulness, both for joyful memories and for the abiding usefulness of all that it had taught them.'

However, Father and Mother not being opulent, I was delighted with my platform in the trees, dreaming, bird-watching or just enjoying the warmth of the leaf-dappled sunshine. As for cooking, I learnt that at home long before I was tall enough to reach the kitchen table. I stood on a stool and was soon promoted to making dainties for Mother's parties. One of my specialities was meringues, and I have passed on the knack to several friends.

In the winter my playroom was a deep recess on the landing. Here I had my dolls' house, made by my brother Algy out of a large wooden stores box. He papered the rooms with pieces left over by house decorators and covered the floors with oilcloth. I cut out pictures from catalogues of furniture, pasted them on to cardboard and painted them. When Algy left school and got a job in an insurance office, he seemed to me terribly affluent. He bought a fretwork machine and made me some really beautiful furniture from patterns in *Hobbies* which he took every month. I had only a penny a week for pocket-money, but for this I could buy one doll about six inches high, or two smaller ones. I dressed them with pieces from Mother's scrap-bag, and several times I had the nerve to go into a draper's shop and ask for half a yard of baby ribbon at a penny a yard so that I could make sashes! Another favourite way of spending my penny was to buy a long strap of licorice for a ha'penny with a ha'pennyworth of sherbet. I would lick the licorice, dip it in the sherbet and suck the fizzy mixture. It was delicious! And it lasted quite a long time.

Alongside the dolls' house was an old trunk where I kept things for dressing-up. Mother would make fairy dresses, outfits for gnomes, etc., out of her old evening dresses. For dressing-up, my little school-friend used to come and play with me, so that we could admire each other. In time we had quite a varied wardrobe, so that we could act the fairy stories that we knew by heart, trailing around in long robes with artificial flowers in our hair.

When I was well into my teens, Mother put into this box, into which I was always rummaging, a book telling me about the facts of life, as they are called. I never discussed the book with Mother, but she knew that I always read and digested anything I could lay hands on, and I think she was quite satisfied that I should not grow up in ignorance of sex.

The End Room downstairs, where the boys used to play, was a scene of great activity. After they got over the white mice stage, which I hated, because the poor little creatures smelt very unpleasant, they made their own railway—rails, trucks and a steam engine, all from bits and pieces. I am sure they got quite as much pleasure from making these things as little boys get nowadays from their elaborate working models of railways. Then they started scientific experiments. They had a tube which split light into all the colours of the spectrum and they had a machine with metal handles which gave us all electric shocks as we held hands round the room. I did not like this much, for though they promised that the shocks would be quite little ones, they could not resist sometimes increasing the power, or whatever it was, so that we all screamed. Algy was greatly interested in wireless telegraphy. He and a doctor friend who lived in the next street rigged up an apparatus and they were soon signalling to each other in Morse code. This must have been shortly after the turn of the century, very early days for wireless discoveries. If Algy had had a scientific training at one of the universities, he would have been in his element. But he got thoroughly fed up with being in an insurance office and emigrated to Canada in his early twenties. I never saw him again and he very seldom wrote to us. The boys from Harlesden College seemed to spread themselves all over the world, as it was the time of our great Empire and there were plenty of interesting openings for them. However, Reg stayed in England and I never lost touch with him.

On Sunday afternoons the boys and I went for long walks, usually to Harrow. There were long stretches of real country between Harlesden and Wembley and between Wembley and Harrow. On the outskirts of Harlesden there was a public house called the Coach and Horses. It was a great thrill when we were passing this pub if the proprietor was preparing to go for a ride in his trap. It was a large trap, with a very strong horse between the shafts, but we held our breath as we saw Jolly Jumbo, as he was called, trying to get into it. He was the fattest man I have ever seen, reputed to weigh 56 stone! Would he get in without pulling the trap over? Of course he always managed it successfully, but when the ostler had closed the door on him he bulged over on all sides. He was a familiar sight in our town, as he took his 'carriage exercise' daily.

I used to take our dog, Conrad, or his successor, Pat, a madly boisterous Irish terrier, for a walk before breakfast every fine morning. I wore Plimsoll shoes and ran most of the time, and covered quite long distances. Sometimes I would get as far as Park Royal, where great preparations were being made for a huge exhibition of the Royal Agricultural Society. The railway was taken there and a special station built, and the exhibition was to be opened by King Edward VII.

Sometimes I would reach Twyford Abbey, and once the gate was open and I saw the monks taking their exercise in the grounds, walking very slowly and with their heads bowed.

Pat was almost frenzied by the sight of water and he would race ahead whenever there was a stream in the offing, then emerge and shake himself all over me and jump up at me with his muddy paws. Once Mother scolded me mildly and said: 'My dear child, I wish you could keep yourself at least clean and tidy. You look like a birch broom in a fit. You never know when Mr Right may come round the corner and he'd get a shock if he saw you like that.' Well, it was a very long time before Mr Right came round the corner, but when he came, oh, how Right he was!

CHAPTER THREE

Christmas

The Christchild stood at Mary's knee,
His hair was like a crown,
And all the flowers looked up at Him,
And all the stars looked down.

GILBERT KEITH CHESTERTON
A Christmas Carol

We spent Christmas at home in the traditional way.
For one thing the winter weather always seemed to be
very cold and snowy, just as our summers were dry
and hot. The boys and I made paper chains to decorate
the rooms. We made the paste out of flour mixed with
a little cold water and added boiling water till it was
transparent. We linked together strips of coloured
paper which were hung from the corners of the rooms
to the centre of the ceilings. Mother decorated the
pictures and mirrors with holly and a large bunch of
mistletoe was hung from the hall lamp. We had oil-
lamps in those days and Father made it his job to keep
them filled and to clean the wicks. Mother made lamp-
shades of pink silk lined with white, and our evenings
were lit with a warm and romantic glow. Nothing like

so labour-saving as electric light, but very cosy all the same.

Mother made Christmas puddings from a recipe handed down from her mother, and they were boiled in the copper for hours and hours, filling the house with a very good smell. One of Father's customers sent him an enormous ham, which was cooked in a large oval cauldron, very different from the dainty pots and pans which are ranged in modern kitchens. Another customer sent Father a couple of pheasants, and it was my job to pluck all the lovely feathers out.

Before my brother Reg became articled to a chartered accountant, he had a job with Miles Birket Foster, the brewers. This firm seemed to me most interesting, for I had a copy of *Poets of the Nineteenth Century*, most of the illustrations to the poems being by Miles Birket Foster, the artist. The contemporary Miles Birket Foster, who was a friend of my brother, was a member of a dramatic society which performed in our church hall G. B. Shaw's *Arms and the Man*, my first introduction to the great playwright. Then one of the directors lived in a lovely house with white-panelled rooms in Paddington which once belonged to Lady Hamilton. Beneath this house were great stables where magnificent dray-horses were housed. They were beautifully groomed and looked after, and each horse had his name on a brass plate over his stall. I expect you wonder what all this had to do with Christmas. Well, it was the custom of the firm each Christmas to give every member of the staff an enormous turkey, weighing 22 lbs upwards. This was much too heavy for Reg to carry home, and it was a great sight to see him and the turkey sharing a hansom cab and jingling up to our door.

Sabey, our baker, sent us an enormous fruit cake, and Welford's, our dairy, gave us a pint of cream. Both these came 'With the Compliments of the Season'. Mother, Annie and I worked hard on Christmas Eve preparing everything possible, so that Mother could come with us to church in the morning. Old Annie stayed home to do the cooking. As soon as we got home from church, aunties and uncles and cousins began to arrive to share the Christmas dinner with us. After the turkey and trimmings the Christmas pudding was brought in, decorated with holly and blazing with burning brandy. Father invariably complimented Mother: 'Better even than last year, my dear, if possible.'

I can't remember that we had much in the way of presents, but I always had a new purse from Father's partner with a golden half-sovereign in it and a book from his sister. I don't think Christmas was so much commercialized in those days, but we had many lovely Christmas cards, and I remember once when my brother Algy became a wage-earner he gave me a great roll of Whatman's Not and Whatman's Hot-pressed paper in many tints, and that morning in my stocking I had had pencils and a box of pastels and rubbers. Rare gifts like this were unforgettable. After dinner we sat round the fire and exchanged all the family gossip. Then a dish of snapdragon was brought in—raisins in blazing brandy—and we made quick dashes to get at the fruit without burning our fingers.

On Boxing Day we had visits from the postman, the greengrocer, the butcher, the baker, the milkman, the laundryman, the little girl who cleaned our doorsteps, the little boy who cleaned our knives, the road-sweeper, the sweep and the lamplighter, all wishing us the compliments of the season and getting their pieces of silver.

We had a small children's party on a Saturday near to Christmas so that Father could be with us. To start with we had the usual games—Kiss in the Ring, Postman's Knock, General Post, Musical Chairs, Poor Jenny is a-Weeping, Oranges and Lemons, Honey-pots, etc., then we had supper. While we were eating, Father was arranging the sitting-room with rows of chairs, hanging a sheet on the wall and preparing a stand at the back of the room for his magic lantern. We trooped in to the warm smell of oil and took our seats. There were panoramic slides showing grotesque

figures, coloured plates showing scenes from fairy
stories, Cinderella, Jack and the Beanstalk, Ali Baba
and the Forty Thieves, the Sleeping Beauty, Blue-
beard, etc. The show finished with some moving
pictures, with figures walking, lifting their hats and
changing their expression. Then there was a kind of
kaleidoscopic effect, and at last Father Christmas wishing us a Happy Christmas. I don't expect it sounds very
exciting to the present cinemagoers, but we thoroughly
enjoyed it, especially when Father put in a slide upside-
down, 'accidentally for the purpose'.

I went to some splendid parties where there were
great Christmas trees touching the ceiling and a little
present for each child, but we never had a family tree
as far as I can remember. However, my little friend
and I sometimes saved up our pennies and bought a
tiny tree for sixpence and had fun decorating it with
things that we made ourselves. Candles were not
allowed because of the risk of fire. We dressed ha'penny
dolls, made baubles from seed-pods covered with
silver-paper, cut out coloured butterflies and flowers
from magazines and had a paper fairy to top the tree.
It made quite a good show. Sometimes Father would
let us play with two of his scientific toys, a kaleido-
scope, an instrument containing loose fragments of
coloured glass and two plane mirrors, so arranged that
changes of position gave an endless variety of sym-

metrical varicoloured forms; and a stereoscope, which had two eye-pieces fixed to a wooden slide with a stand at the end which held two exact pictures side by side a little way apart. When you looked through the eye-pieces the two pictures were combined so that you got the effect of depth and perspective. The photographs were of foreign towns, mountains, landscapes, famous buildings, and the effect was so real that a little girl felt she would like to be small enough to get into the picture and walk about.

Old Annie took me to my first pantomime at Drury Lane. It was called *King Klondike*, which I suppose dates it, and the Dame was played by Dan Leno. I was, of course, thrilled with the experience, and as I always knew by heart any tune and words that I had heard, I shocked my classical parents by singing when I got home:

> Our lodger is a nice young man,
>   A nice young man is he.
> So good, so kind,
>   To all the familee.
> He's never going to leave us,
>   Oh dear, oh dear, No!
> He's such a goody, goody man,
>   Mama told me so.

After this, I went to Drury Lane pantomime for many years, for my little friend's mother, who was a widow, had a box given to her and I was always asked to join the party.

Just before Christmas, when I was six years old, Mother took me to see a magnificent display of dolls at the Albert Hall. The enormous rotunda was stacked with thousands of dolls all the way round. They seemed to represent every country in the world, and were resplendently dressed. I seem to connect the visit in my memory with splendid organ music, Royalty, and Clara Butt singing *Land of Hope and Glory*, but I have not been able to confirm this. However, there is no doubt about the Doll Show, for the following account of it appeared on December 19th, 1896, in the *Illustrated London News*.

TRUTH *Doll Show*

'The seventeenth annual display of dolls and other toys contributed by the readers of *Truth* for the benefit of poor children whose Christmas must perforce be passed in work-house or hospital ward, was opened on Wednesday last at the Albert Hall. It is worthy of record that this charitable institution, promoted by Mr Labouchere and originally held at his editorial offices, has year by year outgrown its head-quarters, passing in succession from the offices of *Truth* to the Marlborough Rooms, thence to the Portman Rooms, and onward, via the Grosvenor Gallery and other temporary quarters, to the great Albert Hall itself. Nor has its annual sojourn in so large a building had a depressing effect on the charitably inclined, for this year's display outdoes all its predecessors, with a total of 29,000 toys for the gladdening of some 28,000 poor children who are at present occupants of the various charitable institutions of the metropolis. The display of dolls included many dressed with great ingenuity, and the groups were strikingly effective, especially one representing Li-Hung-Chang's visit to Hawarden. One of the most strikingly attired of the individual dolls was, appropriately enough, that contributed by Miss Dora Labouchere, which represented a "Mistress of the Hounds" in the orthodox "pink" with hunting horn and whip accoutred. Miss Warburg's ten little figures attired after well-known pictures by the late Sir John Millais have also won much admiration. In addition to the toys, the little people are once again to receive eleven thousand sixpences, fresh from the Mint, the tribute of a child-lover who prefers to remain anonymous; and crackers galore are supplied by Mr Tom Smith.'

CHAPTER FOUR

Holidays

Happiness is large, so large!
All sunlight's holden in its span
All green of trees
All flowers' delight
All scent of moon or starlit night.
The Milky Way binds its expanse
The milkweed spatters its curve with white—
So large, it lets the lover's glance
Hit the high roof of heaven, and then
Come shooting back to earth again;
As well
Happiness swells like a great white curving shell.
JANE BIRKINSHAW: *Happiness*

I don't think that anyone ever had more glorious
holidays than we had every year. The first time I went
to Cornwall I was only four months old, so I don't
remember much about it. I don't know how Father
had discovered St Mawes, for it was then only a small
fishing village and hardly any 'foreigners' went there.
That was in 1890. At first we went by night train so as
not to waste a second of our fortnight. It was non-
corridor, but we stopped at Swindon for a long time

and there were lengthy queues outside the Ladies and Gents on the platform. If we were at the end of the queue we were terrified that the train would go off without us.

But soon we travelled by the wonderful Cornish Riviera express, which was the last word in luxurious travel. The train was drawn by a beautiful green and gold steam engine, kept in a state of spick and span perfection and driven by a loving driver—a worthy steed to take us to the Delectable Duchy. It rolled out from Paddington exactly on the dot of 10.30 in the morning. The train was spotlessly clean, including the loos, the staff were all very friendly and there was a nurse to look after anyone feeling a bit travel sick. The fare was 25s. return for a fortnight, or 30s. if you were staying for a month. For a small sum you could get a ticket which would enable you to travel anywhere by train for a month. Not that we even saw a train once we had got to St Mawes. There were some exciting moments for me on the journey, seeing the swan boats at Dawlish, where we followed the sea coast for a long way, and then the 'dolls' houses' in Cornwall. I did not understand much about perspective, and when crossing the great viaducts above the wooded valleys I found it hard to believe that anyone could really live in the cottages which appeared so tiny in the distance. They seemed only a few inches high.

It was a great moment when we arrived in Falmouth station and saw the lovely harbour full of yachts and steamers and tugs. Our dear old boatman, Nick Odgers, would be on the platform to welcome us. He had his sailing-boat by the steps of the docks, which were then open to the public and close to the station. He and a porter would pile our luggage on a truck and we would soon be on board, so that our holiday started at once. It was lovely to round the Lugo Buoy and see St Mawes once more curving round a cosy inlet in the Falmouth Harbour, thatched, whitewashed cottages along the front with the church on a hill at the back. Mr Dash with a wooden leg and a truck, would meet us on the quay and take our luggage to the Manor House, at the top of Bohella, where we would have a warm welcome from Mrs Hicks. I was always tired after the journey and literally was asleep as soon as my head touched the pillow.

I was wakened early next morning by a tap on the door about half-past six and Father and I would go over to Falmouth on the 7 o'clock steamer, generally the *Roseland*, to fetch the mail. We just had time to dash to Webber's opposite the end of the pier for our early morning cuppa, then back to St Mawes in time for breakfast. Then we would consult with Nick as to which beach would be out of the wind, take a dinghy out to his little sailing-boat and spend the morning on some fine sandy stretch, which we had all to ourselves. We would swim and afterwards play soft-ball beach cricket with driftwood set up for a wicket and another stouter bit for a bat. Then back to St Mawes for dinner, for which we had worked up a good appetite: real— not frozen—meat or poultry, home-grown vegetables and perhaps raspberries and Cornish cream for afters. The cooking was superb, and I think the charge was 25s. a head, all found, for the week, children half-price, though we ate as much as the others.

In the afternoons we would sail to some charming village in the harbour—Mylor or St Just or Flushing, or further out to the Helford River or beyond St Anthony's Lighthouse to Portscatho. During our fortnight's holiday we usually had two longer excursions on one of the St Mawes steamers, the *Alexandra* or the *Roseland*. We would pass Portscatho and the Gull Rock and on to Fowey, Q's lovely village.

Next week we would go to Church Cove, Lizard, and walk to Kynance Cove, a magical place of colourful marbled rocks of olive green, crimson and grey, called serpentine. The sands were golden and the sea was emerald green, which was reflected on the underside of the gulls' wings as they flew over. In those days the walk to Kynance Cove was on top of a hedge dividing the moorland, with exotic scents rising from the heather and the mixture of low-growing flowers.

There were great boulders piled up on the way down to the cove, and sometimes we would have the excitement of seeing a grass snake slithering among the rocks. Nowadays I believe there is a motor-road to the Cove and lots of shanty shops selling ornaments turned from the local stone, postcards and ice-cream. I have not been there for a very long time, but it is in my heart as I used to know it.

When I was twelve or thirteen, our doctor looked me over and said to Mother: 'She whines like a little puppy-dog and is as thin as a skeleton. Next time you go to St Mawes leave her there, let her run wild with the village children and eat plenty of milk chocolate.' I was then still at the dame school, where no fuss would be made if I were absent so long as there was a good reason. So I was left in charge of an old aunt, whom I hardly ever saw, as she took a season ticket for the steamers and stayed on them all the time. I was quite happy playing by myself on the beaches and by the rock-pools. I loved to collect shells and pebbles. It was the habit of the Cornish villagers to throw their broken glass and china into the sea. In time these fragments were worn smooth and round by the action of the waves and were washed up on the beaches like jewels. I would set myself to find so many sapphires, rubies, amethysts and emeralds, and marbles of earthenware and willow-pattern plate. Some of the tiny shells—pale pink cowries, primrose, yellow, gold and brown winkles I left in their natural state—but the tiny conical ones I soaked in a mild solution of acid which was given to me by a couple of artist brothers who were painting in the neighbourhood. The limey outer coating of the shells was eaten away and I was left with varied shapes of pure mother-of-pearl. I had a brilliant 'jewel-box' to take back with me at the end of the holiday, the box itself being covered with the pearly shells.

Gradually I became friendly with all the village children and joined in their swimming and long country walks. I remember once they stole a turnip from a field and cut it up and we each had a bit. I did not care for it, but ate it just to be like the others. When their summer holidays ended I went to the village school with them, until I was told by the master that if I went any more I should have to be registered as a pupil and go all the time. When at last I went home I was as brown as a berry and perhaps I had put on a bit of weight. Anyhow, I had had a very happy, memorable time, and I was delighted to get lots of picture-postcards from little Pascoes, Jenkinses, Greens, Hitchens and Hoopers, all with the same message: 'Hope this finds you well as it leaves me at present.'

Later, when I was at the Haberdashers' School, we were given the most delightful holiday tasks. One was to collect as many different wild flowers as we could, dry them between blotting-paper and stick them in an album. Cornwall was a splendid place for this, and I verified the names from three sixpenny books, *Wild Flowers at Home*, published by Gowans and Gray. I still have them. The parchment covers have gone brown with age, but inside the photographs of sixty flowers in each book are as clear as ever, and they told me all I wanted to know. The nomenclature and order adopted were taken from *Hooker's Student's Flora*, 1884. Another 'task' was to paint a landscape in water-colour. I did a seascape—a little scarlet sailing-boat on a stormy grey sea, with Pendennis Castle in the background, and was given George Eliot's *Scenes of Clerical Life* as a prize.

Sunday in those days in Cornwall was really a holy day. No pleasure- or fishing-boats were on the water, and in the morning practically everyone went either to church or chapel. After breakfast you could see little girls carrying the Sunday joint to the bakehouse to be cooked so that the whole family could go to morning service. We used to go to St Just Church on one of the loveliest creeks in England. We walked along the high road from St Mawes, past the humming telegraph-poles and a little pond where a bush of Rose of Sharon grew over the water, till we turned down a footpath leading to the church. There was a glorious view of the Carrick Roads over a low blackberry hedge on the left, and on the right a field of wheat and poppies and chicory. As we emerged by a farm I was always amused to see the hens perched high in the boughs of a tree. The upper lych-gate was on a level with the top of the tower and the lower lych-gate was often washed by the sea at spring tides. In the porch there was a list of the clergymen going back to the earliest times of recorded history, and the names themselves were full of romance.

The church was founded about A.D. 550 in honour of St Just the Martyr, and it was served from that time until about 590 by Celtic clergy from the adjacent cell of Lanzeague. About 950 it was taken from the Celtic Church by the Saxon Bishops of Cornwall, Crediton and Exeter, who held it until 1140. Then St Just Church was given by Robert, Bishop of Exeter, to the Canons of Plympton Priory and served by their Vicars. In 1189 the Patronage was recovered from the Priory by John le Sor, Lord of Tolverne; thenceforth, after the death of Alvredus, the last Vicar, the incumbents have been Rectors. In 1261 the Church was consecrated by Walter, Bishop of Exeter. Thereafter, the list reads: 1265, William de Sancto Justo; 1282, John; 1297, Philip de Cornubia; 1308, Philip de Careveldros; 1308, Sir Reginald le Seor; 1322, Benedict de Arundelle; 1329, Sir John de Eysi; 1333, Sir Richard de Brankescombe; 1349, Sir Richard Soor; 1383, Sir Thomas Raulyn; and so on.

In the afternoon we generally walked across the fields to the Percuel Ferry, along hedges full of flowers and lovely butterflies—peacocks, meadow browns, commas, fritillaries, red admirals, small coppers, small blues; and the ragwort was covered with a black and red moth or butterfly whose name I don't know. The whole place was a-flutter with them.

From a bridge at the back of the White Cottage in Falmouth where I now live, I can see across the harbour that high road to St Just, and I nearly always pause there and remember our Sundays of long ago, and the great thing was the utter peace and stillness:

> *Das ist der Tag des Herrn.*
> *Ich bin allein auf weiter Flur;*
> *Noch eine Morgenglocke nur,*
> *Nun Stille nah und fern.*
> *Das ist der Tag des Herrn.*

> This is the Lord's day.
> I stand alone on the broad lea;
> One more church bell chimes distantly,
> Then far and wide silence holds sway.
> This is the Lord's day.

The older I grew the more I loved my holidays in Cornwall, and when at long last I married Howard Spring, I longed to take him to my beloved county.

We went there for our honeymoon and walked from Exeter in Devonshire to St Germans in Cornwall, took a train to Falmouth and then by sea to St Mawes. He was enchanted, and later when he came to write his novels, Cornwall appeared in most of them. His description of the beautiful places brought literally hundreds of people to see for themselves, many of them from all over the world—New Zealand, Australia, Canada, Venezuela, America, South Africa—as I know by the letters I have had and by visitors to the White Cottage.

Sometimes, now that I am old and cannot walk very far, my younger son comes from Dorking out of the 'season' and takes me by car to see the old familiar places, which are just as lovely in the winter as they ever were. The sea has washed the golden beaches free of litter, golden gorse grows in every roothold it can find in the craggy rocks and seems never out of bloom; under the winter sunshine the sea is as blue as ever and the white-topped rollers curl in, sometimes quietly, sometimes with giant force.

CHAPTER FIVE

Processions

The King's horses, the King's men,
They march down the street and they march back again,
The King's horses and the King's men.
Some in scarlet, some in gold,
All dollied up they're a joy to behold,
The King's horses and the King's men.
They're not out to fight the foe,
You might think so, but O dear No!
They're out because they've got to go
And put a bit of pep into the Lord Mayor's Show.

Popular Song

Father had plenty of friends in the City who could let us children watch the Lord Mayor's Show from one of their windows overlooking the route. This was a great treat. The floats were beautifully decorated and we loved above all to see the mounted Life Guards.

Not many years ago I was staying in the Savoy Hotel with my husband and we had a River Suite looking on to the Embankment. It was Lord Mayor's Show day and we were doing our bit of packing ready to return to our Cornish home. Suddenly we heard a faint clipperty-clopperty in the distance. The sound came

F.   E nearer and nearer and we looked out to see what it was. There they were, the beautiful Guards, ready to put a bit of pep into the Show. The sight brought back many happy memories.

In 1897 Father and Mother had very good and expensive seats to see the wonderful procession to celebrate Queen Victoria's Diamond Jubilee. They said they had twins at home aged twelve.

'Bring them for the price of one,' they were told.

'And we have a little girl aged seven.'

'She must not miss it; just bring her along.'

But before the great day Mother took me to see the Indians who had come over for the procession. They had an encampment in Hampton Court. It was a calm, sunny day and Hampton Court was a lovely setting. I had never seen Indians before and I thought they looked wonderful with their fine features, slender build and pastel-coloured turbans, like princes out of my favourite fairy tales.

'Are they all beautiful in India?' I asked.

Mother smiled. 'Well, I expect they choose some fine ones to come over to England for the Diamond Jubilee.'

I broke away from Mother and went up to one of them and said 'Salaam!'

'Little Missie been to India?' he beamed.

'No, but I should like to go there.'

At this point Mother caught me up and apologized for her forward little girl.

On the great day we were up at the peep of dawn and in our seats in time to see the soldiers line the route and the carts come along full of golden sand which men threw thickly on the ground. There was plenty to watch and time went like lightning. Hawkers ran along the route selling very long, concertina'd pictorial folders showing the order of the procession and the names of the different contingents. I wish I had mine now but, of course, I threw it away, little knowing how much I should have valued it. It was a magnificent procession, soldiers and sailors from all over the world. I don't suppose there ever had been such a sight before, and certainly it will never happen again. There were heads of all the self-governing colonies; English, Scottish, Irish and Welsh troops, Canadians and Australians, Chinamen from Hong Kong, Dyaks from British North Borneo and, most brilliant of all, Imperial Service troops sent by the native princes of India. The Sikhs had a great ovation.

I shall never forget the great roar in the distance as the much-loved Queen and Empress came along, in an open carriage drawn by eight cream ponies, with outriders and two Indians standing up at the back of the carriage. It was a thrilling moment as I caught sight of her, in a white cap which shone so that I think it must have been sprinkled with diamonds. Of course it was a gloriously sunny day; it always was for her; 'Queen's weather', it was called.

I did not go to Spithead on Saturday, June 26th, when the Prince of Wales reviewed the Fleet. It must have been a magnificent sight, for there were 165 vessels of all classes drawn up in four lines, extending altogether to a length of thirty miles! But many years later Father took me on the Dublin boat to see King George V review the Fleet at Southampton. This boat sailed regularly from London to Dublin, calling in at Southampton and Falmouth. It was a familiar sight to me when I was on holiday at St Mawes, and it looked enormous sailing between Pendennis Castle and St Mawes Castle. When we reached Southampton on the day before the Review, the Captain obligingly anchored just next to the royal yacht. Father and I were on deck early, wondering if the King would appear on his yacht in purple pyjamas trimmed with ermine! We followed the royal yacht at a respectful distance as she went along the lines, and we had a salute from every ship except the German warship. A sign of the times.

Our dear Queen Victoria died on January 22nd, 1901, when I was nearly eleven years old. We had seats to see the funeral procession, and it was a magnificent though sad sight. The coffin was followed by kings and princes from all over the world. Everyone in the crowd wore black, and the shops in London had black boards across and round their windows. Noël Coward caught the mood of mourning wonderfully in his revue *Cavalcade:* ladies in black were walking slowly and solemnly in the park when suddenly a butcher's boy appeared with his blue and white striped apron, whistling merrily, and all the ladies looked shocked.

Apart from these grand national processions, in those days of horse-drawn traffic, and not much of that, we had very good shows in the suburbs. Every year Lord George Sanger's circus came to Harlesden and the near-by towns and advertised their performance by a train of lovely horses, tumbling clowns, elephants in line each holding in his trunk the tail of the one before him, and tall decorated horse-drawn pyramids which seemed to me nearly to touch the sky, each crowned by a beautiful lady.

In 1900, during the Boer War, all the near-by towns —Harrow, Willesden, Kensal Rise, Willesden Green, Harlesden and Neasden—joined forces and had a really magnificent Carnival and Torchlight procession in aid of the *Daily Telegraph* Soldiers' Widows and Orphans Fund. I remember that on the day of the procession I was at the window of an upstairs room facing the street when I was startled to see a horrible face thrust at me. It was a collecting-bag in the form of a mask, held on the end of a long pole by a clown who was scouring the small side streets so as not to miss anyone.

Each town sent a band, there were decorated floats with The Home that Tommy Left Behind Him, floats with widows, another one with orphans, a naval gun with escort, bicycles massed with flowers ridden by ladies in enormous beribboned hats and flowing skirts, the Canterbury Pilgrims, a four-horse stage-coach and a little boy on a horse dressed up as Bugler Dunn, one of the heroes of the Boer War. The procession seemed endless, and altogether £3,000 was collected, a large sum in those days.

As I write I have beside me a Souvenir of the Carnival and Torchlight Procession, with a picture of Kipling's Absent-Minded Beggar on the cover. Many tradesmen in the towns took advertising space to add to the funds, and in the light of today's prices and help-yourself stores they are very amusing. Butchers and dairymen say that families are waited on three times daily, distance no object. The principal grocer in Harlesden advertises a special blend of tea at 1s. 8d. a pound. Tudor and Jenks, the leading drapers, offer Admiralty serges, guaranteed not to spot, shrink or cockle, at 1s. ¾d. a yard. A job master has Broughams for hire, to Theatres, 10s. 6d.; to Balls, 12s. 6d.; to

Town, 10s. 6d. But perhaps best of all, there is a semi-detached villa in Harrow in the most charming and healthy district, two reception, four bedrooms, bath-room, kitchen and the usual offices, finished in the best West End style, good garden, price £460.

CHAPTER SIX

Going to the City

Earth has not anything to show more fair;
Dull would he be of soul who could pass by
A sight so touching in its majesty;
This City now doth, like a garment, wear
The beauty of the morning; silent, bare,
Ships, towers, domes, theatres, and temples lie
Open unto the fields, and to the sky;
All bright and glittering in the smokeless air.
Never did sun more beautifully steep
In his first splendour valley, rock, or hill;
Ne'er saw I, never felt, a calm so deep!
The river glideth at his own sweet will:
Dear God! the very houses seem asleep;
And all that mighty heart is lying still!

WILLIAM WORDSWORTH
Upon Westminster Bridge, September 3rd, 1803

On Saturday morning Father would often take me
with him to the City. This was a great treat. Now, if
Father was going for a long distance by train, he
would be on the platform in very good time, but when
catching the 8.24 to the City he would invariably cut it
very fine indeed. Willesden Junction was about a mile

from our house in Harlesden, and we would fly along at top speed and race down the stairs for the low-level platform from which we caught the Broad Street train. The train would be just about to start, the guard would be looking anxiously up the stairs with his green flag in his hand, he would bundle us into Father's usual carriage, and away we would go.

The carriages were spotlessly clean and very comfortable, with three seats each side, with arm-rests between the seats. The other five occupants were friends of Father's—tycoons, they would be called nowadays. The only one whose name I can remember was a Waterlow, who had to do with paper. Someone would say: 'Cutting it very fine again, Pye,' then they would retire behind their *Financial Times* and their cigars for the rest of the journey, very seldom making a remark. Father would lift up the arm of his seat so that I could snuggle up to him and not steal any of the great men's room. None of the windows was open, the cigars went full puff and I was very glad to get out into the fresh air on Broad Street platform.

I really loved the City, which was practically unaltered since the time of Charles Dickens. It was grimy, but full of history and character. Father's warehouse was up a little alley off Aldersgate Street, leading to Barbican. I was fascinated by the word Barbican, especially when Father told me that it had once been a fortified tower in mediæval times, with a secret passage leading to the churchyard of St Giles, Cripplegate.

The warehouse of George Pratt and Co., Father's firm, was a shabby enough place, with four floors piled up with bales of cotton. As soon as you opened the door you were greeted by that oily smell of cotton with which I was afterwards to become so familiar when I passed through Portland Street, Manchester. Father and his partner, Mr Hudson, shared an office on the ground floor. Mr Wilkinson, who afterwards inherited the business because neither of my brothers was interested in it, would be bustling about all over the place, measuring off lengths from the great Manchester bales and making parcels of the stuff to be taken to their destination by Sam, who was in my imagination the Bob Cratchit of the place. He certainly looked very poor, as if he very well could have done with that whopping great turkey which the reformed Scrooge gave to Bob on Christmas Day. Sam had a sort of large coster's barrow which would be piled up with parcels of cotton to be taken to customers all over the City.

Mr Hudson was a very gentle and quiet man, a bit of a hypochondriac. I had a very soft spot in my heart for him, first because I liked him, and secondly because at Christmas time he always gave me a purse of Russia leather, smelling very good, and inside it would be a

new golden half-sovereign. His sister, whom I never
met, would send me lovely books—*The Daisy Chain*,
The Wide Wide World, *Little Women*, *Say and Seal*,
Queechy, *Melbourne House*, etc. I read them over and
over again. Today, I suppose, they would be con-
sidered 'goody', but they gave me great pleasure.
I wish I had them now, but they were all lost after
my marriage when we moved from Didsbury to
Pinner.

After Father and Mr Hudson had discussed the
morning's letters and orders, Father and I would set
off on a round of his customers, who were nearly all
tie-makers. The fortune of the firm was made by selling
that little bit of lining, called 'swan', which gave the
tie substance. The 'swan' came in great bales from
Manchester, and it had to have exactly the right 'feel'.
I was fascinated to see Father and Mr Wilkinson
handling the stuff and deciding whether it was exactly
what was required.

I had several friends in the tie factories. Father had
extolled to a chosen few of his customers the beauties
of St Mawes, and I can remember the names of at
least three of them who came there regularly when we
were on holiday. Even the partners of the great Manchester cotton firm of Armitage and Rigby were lured
to Cornwall. I think the Armitage family came only
two or three times, but the Rigbys became devotees

and came regularly for generations, in spite of being great globe-trotters. The last time I saw a member of the Rigby family was when I came across a grandson up to the neck in the sea, trying to get his yacht off the rocks where she had drifted from her moorings during a gale.

When we were going the rounds one of my friends would show me how a great pile of 'swan' was topped by a wooden pattern and applied to a circular guillotine rotating at a great speed so that scores of linings were cut in very few seconds. Sometimes I would meet silk weavers from Spitalfields, bringing their beautiful wares for very expensive ties in Reckitt's-Blue cotton drawstring bags. They were Flemish Huguenots who had fled from religious persecution in their own country and had founded a little colony in Spitalfields, where I believe they still carry on their lovely craft.

The bulk of the silk for ties came from Macclesfield, however. I remember later on in life when we lived in Manchester and were visiting our boys at Abbotsholme in Derbyshire, we passed through Macclesfield and the silk mills were pointed out to me. My thoughts flew back to London and the tie-manufacturers there. Howard Spring once wrote an article in the *Manchester Guardian* with a reference to Macclesfield silk ties, which he thought were rather unimaginative. One of the silk firms most magnanimously sent him some splendid ties to disprove his remark. Howard wore the ties and wondered whether it would be worth while running down Copenhagen porcelain, of which he was inordinately fond!

When Father and I had done the rounds of his customers, we returned to Thanet House, his warehouse. In the counting-house, Mr Wilkinson would draw out from under the counter a table made from the wood of Old London Bridge and we would all sit down to elevenses of tea and biscuits. After that we were free for the day. Parallel with Father's little alley there was another little lane with a few old-fashioned shops. One of these belonged to a shoemaker who had a last especially for Father, who loved to have his shoes hand-made to measure. There was also an antique shop, where Father once bought me a heart-shaped silver trinket-box which still occupies the centre of my dressing-table. On another occasion he gave me six Chinese dessert plates which I still have without a single chip. I expect all those shops are now sunk without trace. If these romantic Dickensian little shops were still there before the Second World War, then they were certainly bombed, as all that district was laid low.

Sometimes we would wander down to the Thames to see the Tower Bridge raised to let ships pass, or we would visit St Paul's Cathedral or one of the Wren churches. Sometimes he would take me to Bunhill Fields Burial Ground to see the graves of John Bunyan and Daniel Defoe, and a lady whose tombstone announced that she had had I don't know how many pints of water drawn from her. It may have been gallons; I forget. Once Father took me to see the inside of the Guildhall, which had been prepared for a royal banquet. It was a magnificent sight, with crimson and gold roses and gold plate on the top table dominated by Gog and Magog, the City giants, three long tables on a lower level running down the hall at right angles to the top table, with more lovely roses and silver wine-coolers. At lunchtime we would go to an ABC shop and have always the same food—a poached egg on toast, a piece of currant-bread and a cup of chocolate. Then we would go home via Farringdon Street and buy luscious fruits from the costers' barrows, and probably a few lily bulbs and plants for the garden. And so home to Mother.

Once when we were going the rounds of the customers I was walking rather slowly and limping, because I had hurt my knee in the gymnasium. Father got a bit impatient and said: 'I'll go on. Meet me under the clock.' He hurried off, and there was I, a little girl alone in London. I limped on and could not find a clock. I went on and on for a long way until I found a clock outside a shop, and there I waited. I waited for

such a long time that at last a crowd gathered round
me and asked me why I was there. A policeman came
up and I told him that I was waiting for Father. 'A nice
state he's in,' he said. 'He's been to the police-station
and was just going to begin the round of the hospitals.
I'll tell him I've found you.' It was a great relief to see
Father again, but for long afterwards I had nightmares
of being surrounded by crowds of people with large
heads, staring at me and jeering.

When stocktaking time came, Father, my two
brothers and I would have a lot of homework to do.
In the warehouse Mr Wilkinson had checked all the
bales of cotton to see how much was sold and how
much remained. Father brought home the results of
his research and we all sat round the large dining-room
table with a pencil and note-book. Father would call
out the quantity to be worked out—perhaps $189\frac{1}{2}$ yards
at $3\frac{3}{8}$d. a yard; $1697\frac{1}{4}$ yards at $4\frac{5}{8}$d. a yard, and so on.
We would work hard at our fractions to see who could
be first, and also to see if all our results tallied. Of
course Reg was generally first, being the mathematical
genius, but it was good exercise for all of us. Then
Father could estimate whether the year had been a
good or bad one. Anyhow, in time he was able to buy
a lovely house in St Mawes with a glorious view of
Falmouth Harbour and five acres of garden, and
in time to retire there and live in a very comfortable

style. He had worked hard all his life and well earned his rest.

Once there was a time of great anxiety at Thanet House, as all the buildings on Barbican were on fire. All the bales of cotton were brought out into the alley, and Father stayed in the City all night. Fortunately, the fire stopped just short of Thanet House and did not touch it. When I went up to the City the following Saturday, all I could see through the cracks of a hoarding which had been erected round the devastated area was a mass of burnt and twisted metal; not a wall was standing.

I believe that it was after this great fire that more stringent precautions were enforced and the fire service greatly enlarged. I remember the fire-fighting building by Euston Station, opposite St Pancras church with the caryatids, where you could see the firemen doing wonderful exercises on ladders, and sometimes a fire-engine, drawn by magnificent dapple-grey horses, would rush out. I don't know whether it is still there. If it is, there are certainly no more lovely horses.

When I think of the City, there is no image in my mind of skyscrapers, stockbrokers and hard-headed businessmen. I like to remember the rather dingy, lowly buildings where I had many friends who might have been created by Dickens; the lovely City churches and St Paul's Cathedral; all the gates—Aldgate,

Cripplegate, Moorgate, Newgate, Aldersgate, Bishops-
gate, etc., each with a world of history attached to it;
businessmen who boasted that their word was their
bond. That is the City I shall always love; alas, how
much of it has gone for ever.

CHAPTER SEVEN

Haberdashers'

I have had playmates, I have had companions,
In my days of childhood, in my joyful schooldays.
CHARLES LAMB

When I was fourteen years old, Mother thought that it was high time that I left the local dame school and attended a school where I should have more specialized teachers and more sensible discipline. For one thing, I was always being 'kept in' at Miss Winhall's school for extraordinary reasons. We had to sign our names on a sheet of paper to say that we had not spoken in the cloak-room. I signed the school cat's name as well as my own. As the cat's name was Pomfrey de Lugo Smacksisma, who could resist it?

Another sin for which I was punished was to print one of my exercises instead of writing it; later, I was kept in to print the luggage labels when the Misses Winhall were going on holiday. Each time I had to learn by heart about fifty lines of Shakespeare, and I rather enjoyed this and spouted it to Miss Trissie with a good bass voice for the men and a little piping treble for the women. This, too, was frowned upon. Mother laughed at my peccadilloes, but she thought it was high time I had a change.

The choice was between the Camden Town High School for Girls or the Haberdashers' Aske's Girls' School at Acton. At that time I believe the headmistress of the Camden Town school was Miss Buss, co-heroine of that engaging and well-known quatrain:

> Miss Buss and Miss Beale
> Cupid's darts do not feel.
> How different from us,
> Miss Beale and Miss Buss!

Our family doctor's niece, Zoë Woodroffe, went to the Haberdashers', and as she lived quite close to us Mother decided to try and get me in there. I was rather frightened at the thought of going to a large school, but after the first week or two I thoroughly enjoyed myself. It was strange at first, for instead of sitting at a table on forms we each had our own private desk, and at half-term we had to change places so that we should not grow up lop-sided.

In addition to a form-mistress, we had a different mistress for every subject. Our head was Miss Margaret Gilliland, a splendid person and the first woman to become an MA of London University. There were about five hundred of us girls in the Upper and Lower school and about forty mistresses to look after us. We

had an extremely efficient matron, a jolly fat cook to
see to our midday meal and several servants, as well as
a groundsman. When I told a modern schoolmarm
about our domestic staff: 'Those were the days!' she
said. Dinner tickets (and we had a very good meal)
were ninepence each, or eight shillings a dozen; and
a profit was made so that lovely reproductions of
famous pictures were bought for the dining-room and
for our classrooms. Another source of income for our
school pictures was the Pound. If we left anything
lying out of place it was impounded and we had to
pay a penny to redeem it. Being the star artist of my
form, I was allowed to choose our two pictures, and I
remember them to this day—Hobbema's *Avenue* and a
delicately-coloured Japanese print of a spray of wistaria
drooping over a pond with a fish looking up at it from
the water.

One Speech Day, the Lord Mayor of London came
to give away the prizes. After the ceremony was over
it was thrilling in our conventual establishment to see
the Lord Mayor's coachman in all his splendid rig-out
with his arm round the waist of Emily, the cook. I
expect he was saying thank-you for a jolly good meal.

In 1904, when I first went to this school, the fee was
three guineas a term, and this fee was remitted for any
kind of outstanding work by a pupil.

Our mistresses were all MA's of some university or

another, and on Prize Day they streamed on to the platform wearing colourful gowns and hoods, excepting Miss Linnell, the language mistress and deputy head. Though she had gained the Modern and Mediæval Language Tripos at Cambridge University, women were not then given a degree, whatever their achievements.

Miss Boyd, who taught us English literature, was most concerned that we should all appreciate the beauty of the spoken word. We could study for ourselves the procession of writers with their dates from the beginnings to the present day in Stopford Brooke's *Primer of English Literature*, but she would spend the whole of the lesson reading aloud to us from Tennyson, Wordsworth, Keats, Shelley and, of course, Shakespeare. I shall never forget her readings from Coleridge's *Ancient Mariner* and *Kubla Khan*. She implanted in me a love of poetry which has lasted all my life. Miss Kate Blackstock, too, opened magic casements for us in the history lesson, and I loved her dearly. Discipline was very strict, but I don't think we were any less happy for that. Every Monday morning Miss Gilliland read out from her dais in the Great Hall a list of forms with no conduct or inattention marks for the previous week, and another list of forms with no absentees. Practically every week, the list was complete, and it really was a great punishment to do anything which took your form off the list. I was away from school for one day only during the time I was there, and that was because I had a badly poisoned foot. Before it was really healed I limped to school in a shoe cut open to accommodate the swelling.

One day when we were in the playground during break, a girl spoke to a boy over the garden wall. I shall never forget seeing Miss Gilliland rushing to-wards them like an angry little galleon, her large brown taffeta sleeves flowing behind her like sails. I'm afraid that girl's form was taken off the list that week.

I was once summoned to Miss Gilliland's study, and I wondered what was up. I was very sentimental about Miss Blackstock, and in a gold tiepin which I wore there was a little secret place in which I had put my beloved's initials. This had fallen to the floor and had been taken to Miss Gilliland. She tore me off a strip, as they say in the Navy. I was a silly, sickly, sloppy, sentimental girl and I ought to be ashamed of myself. She really hissed at me, but I got the brooch back minus the initials, and to my great relief I was not given a conduct mark. And I went on loving Miss Blackstock.

She came to see me in Manchester when my first-born was about a year old, and they played together like a couple of kittens, until David was almost hysterical with laughter. It was a red-letter day for me

The last time I saw her was in 1940, sitting on Paddington platform, and I was very sad but proud because David had just volunteered for the Navy. He was in his first term at Pembroke College, Oxford. Lately I had a letter from an ex-headmistress, who was a younger contemporary of mine at the Haberdashers'. She said that she and most of her friends were 'gone' on Miss Blackstock. She had that intangible magic quality called 'charm'.

Miss Gilliland had a remarkable memory for faces. She met our parents and brothers on Sports Day and did not forget them. My father told me that he met her a few years after I left school on the steps of St Paul's Cathedral and she continued the conversation where they had left off the last time they met at a Sports Day, which is pretty remarkable when you consider that there were so many girls in the school.

She seemed to know everybody in London and took us for some most interesting outings. We went to St Paul's Cathedral and afterwards had tea with Arthur Foley Winnington Ingram, Lord Bishop of London, in a house which he had in St Paul's Churchyard. She knew the Headmaster of Eton, and took us there. We were in the grounds when the roll was called, and the Eton boys looked through us as if we were non-existent. How superior to the Harrow boys, I thought, who always greeted me with wolf-whistles when I passed them in the streets of Harrow.

I should have left the Haberdashers' when I was eighteen years old, but I loved it so much that, as I was working for the Art Class Teacher's Certificate of the Royal Drawing Society, I pleaded with the Head to stay for another year. That last year I was in a small study with a carpet on the floor, a table with chairs round it and a vase of flowers on the table. There were about six of us, the others going in for their Inter BA, and the Head was our form-mistress. We were all very grown-up, with skirts nearly touching the floor, and our hair up and kept in place with a number of hairpins which would keep tumbling out.

I left when I was nineteen years old, and a fortnight later my mother died.

CHAPTER EIGHT

Dancing

All night have the roses heard
  The flute, violin, bassoon.
All night has the casement jessamine stirr'd
  To the dancers dancing in tune,
Till a silence fell with the waking bird
  And a hush with the setting moon.

                    ALFRED, LORD TENNYSON

There was no room at Miss Winhall's school for drill or gymnastics, but Harlesden College, where my brothers attended, had a properly fitted gymnasium, with ribstalls, rope-ladders, ropes for climbing, parallel bars, vaulting-horse, window-frames and poles, ropes and mats for the high jump. There was a class for girls and I attended it with most of my schoolmates, and we enjoyed it very much. We had a drill-sergeant, very Scottish, called Mr McPherson. Sometimes there was a joint display by boys and girls for the benefit of parents, and it was fun seeing my brother Reg and the headmaster's daughter, Margy McKee, competing for the high jump. I think they could both do six feet with a springboard, and then it was a question of competitive inches. I can remember them standing under the rope after they had jumped over it to show that they had jumped more than their own height.

On Monday evenings we all went to dancing-class there, and Mrs Bedford, who taught us, was supposed to be the best teacher of ballroom dancing in London. She had an assistant with a wooden leg, called Miss Dagnall, who was also a very good teacher, though she was a bit heavy to waltz with. When we arrived on Monday evenings, some French chalk was sprinkled over the floor and then we had a good time sliding about on it until it got a good polish. When Mrs Bedford arrived we stood in two rows, boys one side and girls the other, and we made our curtseys and bows to her. I became so used to this that one day when I unexpectedly met her coming round a big rock in the middle of Kynance Cove in Cornwall, I instinctively dropped my best curtsey, though I was wearing beach shoes and swimsuit.

First, we did the steps very slowly, still in line, counting aloud, then we did them to music, and when we had them off by heart Mrs Bedford would say to the boys: 'Will you please take your partners for the waltz,' or whatever it might be. Each boy would bow in front of the girl he wished to dance with and say: 'May I have the pleasure?' It was all very decorous, and white gloves were insisted on. Father, Mother and my brothers went to the late class, and when I was in my teens I was allowed to stay on so that I could go home with the family. We danced the polka, the waltz, the schottische, the valeta, the Lancers and the waltz cotillion. Father and my brothers were first-rate dancers, so I was never without a partner, and my brothers' friends were kind to their young sister.

The first Christmas after we reached our eighteenth year we 'came out'. After that we went to subscription dances, to the tennis-club dance, and the parents of some of my school friends gave dances to which I was invited because of my two useful brothers. My brother Algy had joined the London Rifle Brigade, and I went with him to his regimental ball in town. For the first winter after we 'came out' we wore white low-necked gowns with a train which we hitched up by a loop on a finger when we were dancing. In fact, much as novels sneer at suburban dances, I am sure we had quite as much fun as society débutantes, and the etiquette was just as rigidly observed. We had long white gloves to the elbow, and I remember when Reg had to miss the first two dances because I had forgotten my gloves and he kindly went and fetched them from home. We had little folded programmes with a tiny pencil attached by a silk cord. It was very exhilarating when all the dances had been booked and our dance cards were full. We generally kept a few Extras empty 'just in case'.

The music was provided by a three-piece orchestra, at which Kay Hammond so charmingly scoffed in Noël Coward's *Private Lives*—I can still hear her delicious throaty voice saying: 'A three-piece orchestra at Budleigh Salterton!'

I once listened to a radio item called 'Those Were the Days'. They played a steady *Tum*, tum, tum, *Tum*, tum, tum in a very boring fashion. It was not a bit like that. It was a time of wonderful musical plays such as *The Merry Widow* and *The Chocolate Soldier*, and they all had lovely waltz tunes which were played with feeling and expression. We had first-rate Viennese waltzes by the classic Strausses, father and son, and there was good music by modern composers, such as Archibald Joyce, Oscar Straus, Ivor Novello and Noël Coward. For the Lancers we had adaptations of popular tunes from the current musical plays. The Lancers were jolly, and the waltzes were dreamy and romantic.

For my sins I once heard a real modern dance band with some sort of magnification of sound which nearly broke my ear-drums, though I am a bit deaf. The tunes had about as much romance as a concrete block!

When I was in my late teens, though still at school, my romantic soul was so worked upon that my evening was made or marred by the answer to the question: 'Would *He* ask me to have the supper dance with him?'

He generally did and I was in a state of bliss. Yes, there was a *He*, though I may say at the outset that he never cared for me one scrap. I had known him since I was a toddler, as he was a friend of my brothers. When I was very young he was very rude to me and said he would not come to the house unless the sorrowful little she-bear was chained up, my name being Marion Ursula, which I believe means sorrowful she-bear. But as I grew older he became more kind to me. He took me for my first ride in a motor-car, and it was a wonderful experience flying through the air at thirty miles an hour! He took me to watch him rowing at the Thames Rowing Club. He and his parents came to St Mawes when we were on holiday there and he took me rowing on the Percuel River and spouted Greek poetry at me, which I thought was music of the gods, as I suppose it was. Of course, I did not understand a word of it, and he may have been saying awful things.

Why did I set my young heart on him? Well, he went to Cambridge and I thought undergraduates were marvellous beings in those days. I do not think so highly of students nowadays. His parents seemed to me rich beyond the dreams of avarice, because they had a most wonderful garden with a first-rate gardener and an under-gardener, an aviary, a fern-house, a hot-house, a temperate house and a conservatory opening from the drawing-room, always kept filled with exotic plants in the pink of condition. In fact, I suppose all young girls set their hearts on someone, and he was the most eligible *parti* of our acquaintance.

After I left school and my mother died, I kept house for my father for a year or so. Then he married again and I was most unhappy at home, as I felt I was disliked by my stepmother and not needed by my father. I longed to leave home, and marriage would have been one way out. But my one-sided romance ended abruptly. I was walking along the front in St Mawes having just emerged from the sea, my long hair dripping all round me, looking not only like a birch broom in a fit, but a drowned one into the bargain. To my horror I saw Him coming in the opposite direction with a beautiful girl dressed up to the fashionable nines on his arm. When I got to my room, I shed a few tears, washed my face, and that was that. His engagement was announced the next day and I never saw him again. My great consolation was that I don't think anyone in the world, not even my brothers, knew that I had a tenderness for him. And there had never been any 'petting'. Elizabeth Bennett was my model, not her younger sisters!

I determined to earn my living and get away from what once had been my dearly loved home as soon as possible. If I had only known it, I expect my Guardian Angel was saying to me: 'Cheer up! Be a good girl and work hard and keep your pecker up! If you wait long enough I have got something very much better than him in store for you.' But my dancing days were over.

I asked Father if I might go to Kensington College to train for secretarial work, as I thought it would be a very long time before I could be independent as an artist or art teacher. He consented, and I really worked very hard for the next few months, practising my shorthand on every possible occasion. When my stepmother heard that there were boys at the college, she said to me, quite unnecessarily: 'If I ever catch you having anything to do with boys, I will turn you out of the house at once.' I am afraid my retort was not very polite. Boys, indeed! I had no use for boys, and I don't think I ever spoke to one of them, and never even glanced at them. But I did find at the college a fine lifelong friend, Edith Milnes, whom I always called Milly.

CHAPTER NINE

Going Abroad

Go forth to seek: the quarry never found
Is still a fever to the questing hound,
The skyline is a promise, not a bound.

JOHN MASEFIELD

When the summer holidays came from Kensington College, I went abroad to a family living in Brest, where there was a little girl whose parents wished her to learn English. I wished to become fluent in speaking French. I crossed at night from Southampton to St Malo and slept so soundly that I cannot remember much about the trip. When I woke up we were just passing the Channel Islands. I shared a cabin with some other ladies. I was just going to have a good wash before dressing when one of these women warned me never to wash my face in water when travelling abroad, but always to use face cream and tissues. 'It's safer. You never know what you may catch. And never on any account drink water. It might make you very ill. And if you are offered wine where you are going, don't refuse it; it is much cheaper than Vichy water.' I had told her that this was my first trip abroad and that I was going to stay with a French family, and I think she felt that I needed a bit of motherly advice.

When I landed at St Malo I felt absolutely bewildered, for I was surrounded by cab-drivers and porters who wished to take my luggage. As they all spoke at once I could not understand a word they said. A nice young English boy saw my confusion and rescued me and saw to my luggage. He told me that I could part with my luggage without any misgivings. If it was properly labelled it would go to my destination without any further trouble on my part. Then he gave me a cup of coffee on the pavement outside a café. As I was sitting there there was a great jangling of bells, and I was amazed to see a little steam train hurtling through the streets with quite a string of coaches.

Then the nice boy took me to St Malo station and put me on the wrong train. Instead of going to Brest, it was heading for goodness knows where. However, I was told that I could change at Rennes and get another train to Brest from there. As I had a Cook's ticket, it seemed that I could travel anywhere with it, without any extra charge. There was a very long wait at Rennes, so I went for a walk and had a look at the town. By the river there were a good many women doing their washing, soaping their linen and banging it on the smooth stones, then rinsing it in the running stream. I felt that I had been in foreign parts for ages, what with the pavement café, the little street train and now the washerwomen by the river. I caught my train to Brest all right and arrived very late. The family had been anxious about me, but my luggage had arrived before me, and all was well.

I did not meet the family that night, but was shown into a bedroom which had no windows. It was rather like a very large cupboard, and as I had always been used to sleeping with my windows open as wide as they would go, I felt a bit stuffy. My covering was a huge bag of feathers which I tried to balance on top of me, but it was no good: it slid to the floor. However, I was so sleepy after my exciting journey that I had a very good night, and before I knew where I was Mme Istin brought the whole family to be introduced to me —M. Istin, Charlot, Berthe and two friends, Georges and Robert Godoc. I was not used to receiving visitors in my bedroom and, like Alice in Wonderland, I felt that life was getting curiouser and curiouser.

They left me to dress in peace after I had shaken hands with every one of them, and then a glorious smell of beeswax and turpentine wafted into my room. When I went down to breakfast a manservant in carpet slippers was polishing all the floors, first putting on the wax, then sliding all over the place with a little brush under his foot. My breakfast was a huge *tartine*, which was a thick slice of bread cut from a great round loaf with about a quarter of a pound of butter on it, and a large bowl of coffee with a *crème* floating on top of it. It was all delicious, but oh so rich!

After breakfast, Mme Istin took me to see the market-place, where women in Breton costume were displaying their wares under great coloured umbrellas. A maid-servant called Grosse Aline followed us with a basket into which Mme Istin put all her purchases. I was amazed to see great ripe peaches for *deux sous* apiece. Everywhere we went we saw French army officers, looking so much like the little tin soldiers which I used to buy for a penny a box. It soon became evident that we met the same little officer every time we turned a corner, and when at last he stopped before us and with a deep bow presented me with a bouquet of flowers, Mme Istin insisted that I should have Georges on one side of me, Charlot on the other and Grosse Aline bringing up the rear, as if I were something very precious that might be spirited away. After that I was not even allowed to go a few yards from the house to post a letter without a manservant following me. Used as I was to my free-and-easy life with my brothers and their friends, it seemed very strange.

Georges Godoc's mother was a fine pastry-cook, and it was to her shop that we went for our midday meal.

The food was very rich and there were many courses, followed by another great bowl of coffee with a *crème* on top. I was expected to eat another huge meal in the evening, but I could not have managed another mouthful for a fortune. Mme Istin was most distressed and sent for a friend who could speak English. She explained to me that Mme Istin had told her that I was pining for home and was very worried that I was missing a meal. 'They are very kind people,' she said, 'and they are most unhappy that you eat nothing. Please don't be sad.' I told her that I was very happy indeed, but that I was not accustomed to such large meals. But however much I smiled at her, Mme Istin had many misgivings about my lack of appetite!

Little Berthe was about fourteen years old, very spoilt and with not the faintest intention of learning a word of English, however much I tried to speak to her. I felt I was not earning my keep, but it was no good. The boys took my French in hand and worked hard at my vocabulary. Georges made a list of everyday English words with their French equivalent—metals, precious stones, games, buildings, materials, clothes, birds, animals, fishes, and so on, and heard me say them after I had learnt them by heart. I seemed to give satisfaction, for they said: '*Elle n'est pas comme les autres,*' whoever the *autres* may have been.

At first they all called me 'Mees', but when I explained that it was not the custom in England, they asked me what they should call me. I said: 'Marion, or Miss Marion;' whereupon they all burst into song:

> *Gaie, gaie, marions-nous,*
> *Mettons-nous dans la misère.*
> *Gaie, gaie, marions-nous,*
> *Mettons-nous la corde au cou.*

This was not very flattering to the holy state of matrimony, but they could not resist the pun on my name Marion and *marions*—let's get married.

The only English words with which they seemed at all familiar were 'football', 'half-back' and 'Black and White', but Georges, who was about my age, made very good progress. Berthe, Robert and Charlot would have nothing to do with learning in the holidays. I had to give them up in despair.

If I had been a paying guest, they could not have taken more trouble to give me a good time. We went to a *Pardon* festival at Concarneau, where the women wore the most beautiful and picturesque costumes with coifs; to Quimper to see the fishing fleet and the pottery for which the place was famous; to the harbour where the soldiers were embarking for Algeria, great *miches de pain*, huge circular loaves, strapped to their knapsacks and their weeping families saying goodbye to them. We went to a picnic in the grounds of a beautiful château. The picnic meal was most elaborate. Some of us went in a trap, and the rest followed in a large cart with stove, masses of food, tables, chairs, knives and forks, etc., so that we could have as many courses as we had at home. We picked mushrooms, which M. Istin cooked himself. Mme Godoc attended to the chickens, which seemed to me to be cooked in pounds of butter, and the meal was topped up with the usual great bowl of coffee and *crême*.

The Istins had a little field where they kept a pony, called Mouton, which drew the trap when we went abroad. There was also a big black carriage dog, called Dragon. Mouton had no saddle, but we all tried a bit of bareback riding. Of course I got thrown at once and acquired a fine horseshoe-shaped bruise on my arm, but no bones were broken. I hoped the horseshoe was for luck! If we were riding along country lanes in the trap and Mme Istin saw another vehicle coming from the opposite direction, she started screaming at the top of her voice and continued to scream until we had got safely past. What M. Istin said to her was best not translated, and what she would have done if she had seen one of those dreadful new inventions called an *automobile* I shudder to think. Anyhow, it was a mercy that Mouton did not bolt whenever he heard the piercing screams.

After about a week we youngsters were all packed

off to the Istins' country house at Ploudalmézeau, on
the tip of Finisterre, for our real summer holiday. The
house had no carpets and it was scrubbed every day
from top to bottom by a Breton peasant woman. But
the fleas! Every evening the boys went to all our bedrooms with a huge tin of 'le Keatings' and thoroughly
peppered our beds.

When we were settled in, M. and Mme Istin returned to their affairs in Brest and we were left to a
free-and-easy life, much like my holidays in Cornwall.
There was no more stuffiness, for the house was open
to the sea. Our food was plainer, with lots of beautifully cooked fresh fish and good French bread and
butter. It suited me much better than the rich and too
plentiful meals of Brest. The boys hired a boat to go
fishing, and Berthe and I went with them. They had
not the remotest idea how to sail a boat, but just went
straight to their objective, whatever the wind was
doing. I don't know what my menfolk or Nick Odgers
would have thought of it. The sails flapped and the
boat wobbled from side to side. I don't know how we
did not run on to the rocks, for there were plenty of
them. However, we had good fishing. It was exciting
to look over the side to the seafloor of white sand.
Suddenly from under the sand the shape of a plaice or
sole would show, and we could see them take our bait.
The boys took pride in cooking the fish to perfection

in lots of butter. At the week-ends, Mme Istin would come from Brest with fresh supplies of food, and she proudly showed me fourteen pounds of butter which we youngsters were supposed to consume in a week!

The coast was rather like Land's End, with dangerous-looking rocks and beaches of snow-white sand. In the fields along the sea-shore there were large piles of seaweed—*goémon*—which the farmer-fishermen harvested and from which they extracted iodine and used the dried powdered weed for fertilizers. I was told that they were very prosperous, as not only were they farmers, fishermen and *goémoniers*, but they also took in summer visitors. I was also told that they kept their wealth very secret, burying their gains in the earth. Their farmhouses were guarded by very fierce dogs, and I was instructed to shout '*Da gousket!*' at them if they came for me. I suppose it meant: 'Go back to your kennel!' Anyhow, it seemed to work and I was not savaged. We bathed in the sea every day, and once I had the joy of watching a Breton girl who was preparing for a swim take off her coif, under which was a little cap. When she removed this, her pale golden hair flowed around her to the ground like a mantle, and I thought of Rapunzel. She was very lovely and I could not take my eyes off her.

Once I saw a good display of French temperament, which rather frightened me. I had a little grey satin motoring bonnet trimmed with tiny pink roses and with a floating grey veil. Berthe rather fancied this and took it to a milliner in Brest to be copied. The milliner evidently thought that my bonnet was too modest, for she made a most flamboyant creation, rather like a sunbonnet, in bright blue silk trimmed with red roses. When M. Istin was walking with us in a country lane at the week-end, he went ahead with little Berthe. Evidently they had a difference of opinion, for suddenly he snatched her bonnet from her head, threw it into the road and stamped up and down on it, his face convulsed with rage. I was flabbergasted and I suppose I looked very much upset, for they all came round me and assured me that it did not mean a thing, but poor little Berthe was crying and needed comforting much more than I did. They straightened her bonnet as best they could and soon all was calm once more.

After the holiday when I went back to England, I was put in charge of two young French girls who were going to stay with an English family. We had a very pleasant Channel crossing. We were allowed to stay on deck as it was very calm. We wrapped up warmly and dozed in the bows, and for breakfast we had cold chicken, rolls and butter and fruit which we had brought with us.

As we passed through the English countryside, I could not help feeling how much prettier the cottages looked, so cosy with their thatched roofs, orchards and little gardens full of flowers. The Breton cottages were four-square, with no gardens.

I had a letter every day from Georges until he announced that Maman had arranged a marriage for him, when the correspondence tailed off. Poor Georges! I wonder what became of him. He was doing his *service militaire* at Mont Valérien, and the date was 1913.

CHAPTER TEN

Looking for a Job

Truly one thing is sweet
Of things beneath the sun;
This, that a man should earn his bread and eat
Rejoicing in the work which he hath done.

JOSEPHINE PRESTON PEABODY

On returning to Kensington College after my holiday in Brittany, I found that I had passed my Chamber of Commerce and Society of Arts examinations in short-hand, typing, book-keeping, English, French and German, and I was promoted to the Model Office, under the eagle eye of the proprietor of the college, Mr Munford. It had all the proper paraphernalia of a 'real' office, with filing cabinets, copying machines, telephone to attend to and the boss's desk, and I had to deal with the college correspondence. Once we had reached this stage, we were guaranteed a job.

It was not many days before I was sent out to inter-view a Conservative MP who wanted a secretary. He lived in Park Lane in one of those lovely houses delightfully illustrated by Anthony Gross in the omni-bus edition of Galsworthy's *Forsyte Saga*. I felt a bit nervous, but he was a very pleasant man and soon put me at my ease. He gave me dictation and I managed to transcribe it quite easily, but then came the rub.

'How old are you?' he asked.

I said I was twenty-three.

'I'm sorry,' he said, 'but you see I have to travel about the country a good deal with my secretary. If I engaged you, I'm afraid I should have to engage a chaperone as well, which would come a bit expensive. So I'm afraid . . .'

Well, there it was. As I left his room I saw a very charming-looking middle-aged lady waiting her turn to be interviewed. I hope she got the job.

A few days later I went to an Anglo-American tobacco company in the City. I thought the situation and the building were rather grim, and the office was one huge room with lots of tables with girls at type-writers and lots of 'Munseys' dictating to them. 'Munsey' was a name Milly and I had invented for the kind of wonderful-looking young man who was pictured in *Munsey's Magazine* to advertise American shirts and collars. Oh, those lovely magazines of the early years of the century—the pale blue *Strand*, the pale green *Windsor*, the yellow *Pearson's*, the *Wide World*, the American *Harper's* and *Munsey's*. There is nothing like them nowadays. I still have some early *Strands* with the Sherlock Holmes stories in them.

To return to the Anglo-American tobacco company. One of the Munseys gave me a dictation test and I read it back to him with ease. However, I was not engaged there and then, but was told that I should hear from them later. I thought that that was final. The next day I went to Radium Limited, saw the boss, Mr Mortimer Iles, and was engaged straight away at the magnificent salary of £1 a week. It was a gay, light office right in the heart of the West End, fine for window-shopping! The next morning I had a letter from the Anglo-American tobacco company, asking me to report for duty the next Monday. However, I was by then committed to Radium Limited, and very much preferred the office and the situation. There was only one other secretary, a very pleasant girl. I have always hated to be one of a crowd.

Radium Limited was the pet of a German Professor whose name I forget, though he sometimes came to the office. He had invented an apparatus which was supposed to cure rheumatism. There was a glass bottle filled with distilled water, and in the middle was a perforated container filled with powder which was supposed to emanate so many maché units of radium each day. A dose of this was to be taken by the patient internally. Then there were little satin bags filled with radium powder for external application to the affected part. The bottle was hired out at so much a week, and the little bags were sold.

With my fairly fluent French and smattering of German, my first fortnight was spent in the Imperial Institute, where an International Congress of Medicine was being held. I had a stall with the apparatus and the little bags and had to explain their use to interested foreign doctors. It was rather fun. Next to me a nice English boy had a stall with all kinds of powerful illuminated microscopes. We soon chummed up, as there really was not much doing and we could be on duty as soon as a doctor hove in sight. He showed me some wonderful slides. He scraped a little moisture from one of his teeth, fixed it in a slide and showed it to me under one of his most powerful microscopes. It was really quite terrifying. If you can imagine an animated Hieronymus Bosch picture, that was it—all kinds of horrifying animals swallowing smaller animals and dividing and doing devilish tricks. And to think that we have that in our innocent mouths all the time!

At the end of the first week he brought his father to be introduced to me; at the end of the second he asked me to go home with him to meet his mother. But I was terribly keen to continue with my 'career' at a pound a week, so we parted good friends and that was the end of that.

When I started routine work in the office in Mortimer

Street there was not much to do at first, except to take down by telephone a whole string of stock exchange prices. However, there was not a dull moment, as our room faced the Three Arts Club next door and our window was exactly opposite the window of their big practice hall. There we saw Pavlova drilling her *corps de ballet* and doing exercises at the bar which went all round the room. Then there were rehearsals of a musical comedy chorus, and we knew all the tunes by heart long before the opening night. Later, we saw an actor, I think it was Dennis Eadie, trying to get Gladys Cooper to contort her beautiful classic face into an expression of savage rage as she plunged a long pair of tailor's scissors into the imaginary back of a victim. He showed her how to clutch the scissors with real angry passion, but for a long time she persisted in picking them up delicately, as if she were going to use them to cut out a paper pattern! And her face would not express real rage! I expect it was all right on the night. I don't remember which play it was.

During the lunch-hour there were often services in the lovely church of All Saints, Margaret Street, which was close by. Men sat on one side of the church and women the other. There was glorious music, which always sent me half-way to heaven, and little boys swung censers of incense. I was so overcome one day by the music and the incense that when I got back to

the office and went into the boss's office to take dictation, I fainted gracefully into his arms! I was not given
to fainting; it never happened before nor did it after,
but there it was.

All of a sudden there was a great rush of business.
A duke and several other people wrote to the papers
saying what wonderful cures they had experienced
since taking the radium emanation water and wearing
the little pads. Working as hard as we could, we could
not cope with all the correspondence, and Mr Iles
asked me if I knew of anyone who could give us a hand.
I telephoned my friend Milly, who had been at
Kensington College with me, and she came. This
started a real friendship which lasted unbroken until
her death. She did not need the money but wanted
something to do, and it helped to pay for her riding
in Hyde Park at the week-ends. Until her marriage,
we spent all our holidays together, either in Cornwall
or Deal, and as many week-ends as we could manage,
making the beautiful little hamlet of Friday Street in
Surrey our headquarters. We loved the same novelists
and poets, and when a new Georgian Poetry Book was
coming out we almost waited on the doorstep of the
shop in Devonshire Street. We often had lunch at a
vegetarian restaurant next door to the Poetry Book
Shop, run by the sisters of Canon Richmond—a three-
course meal for about ninepence. Once when we

emerged we had the joy of seeing a brace of pheasants delivered by the postman to the Poetry Book Shop, and Harold Monro himself, the editor of the Georgian Poetry Books who lived above the shop, came to the door to take them in. Such were our small delights.

After Milly left Radium Limited she took various secretarial posts until her marriage, and invariably while she was working for him her boss got knighted— she was engaged by a Mr and before she knew where she was she was working for a Sir. One of them was Sir Arthur Yapp of the YMCA. I cannot remember the others. I was a bit jealous, for none of my bosses was knighted. And when I got married to Howard Spring, even he was not knighted, though his books gave delight to millions of people all over the world. The people who decide these things seemed to prefer jockeys, trainers, cricketers and football managers. I never discussed the matter with him, but I don't believe he would have accepted a knighthood. What I am sure would have pleased him would have been to have received an honorary degree of literature at one of the great universities.

One red-letter day for me, the firm of Radium Limited decided to advertise. Harold Dore from the London end of the *Manchester Guardian* came to write the 'copy'. He dictated it to me, and this was one of the turning-points of my life. Before I knew where I was I was working for the advertisement department of the *Manchester Guardian*, and in my spare time doing work for the editorial side. Directly I got into that office over the Post Office in Fleet Street, I felt that I had come home.

CHAPTER ELEVEN

Fleet Street

The man must have a rare recipe for melancholy, who can be dull in Fleet Street.

CHARLES LAMB: Letter to Thomas Manning, 1802

I knew something about the *Manchester Guardian*, because when I was at the Haberdashers' Miss Gilliland had advised the older girls to read the *Daily Telegraph* and the *Manchester Guardian*, so that we could be acquainted with both the Conservative and the Liberal points of view. The bill-posters of both papers were always displayed in the Great Hall. Just as we had to change the position of our desks every half-term so that our bodies should not grow lop-sided, so she hoped that our minds would be trained to look at both sides of a question and not become unreasonably biased.

When Harold Dore, the Parliamentary correspondent, asked me to go to work for the *M.G.*, I told him that I was Conservative to the backbone. He laughed and said: 'So are we all at the London end. I don't think you will find much to quarrel with.' And I never did. A few Left intellectuals drifted in occasionally from the London School of Economics to dictate a London Letter paragraph or so, but I regarded them as incidental and inhuman, probably lots of brain, but no heart or intelligence. I remember when I, glowing with happiness, went to say goodbye to G. D. H. Cole, who was in the office, and told him that the next day I was going North to be married, he said in an icy, thin-lipped voice: 'I hope they will get someone equally efficient to take your place.' There's humanity for you!

Most of the work I did for the advertisement department I did mechanically. I have always been extremely sceptical about advertisements, except those sent out by plant nurseries and seedsmen. But I loved the work for the editorial side. James Bone, the London Editor, was also the art critic. His brother, Sir Muirhead, was a founder member of the New English Art Club, and he did the finest etchings of his time. I began to take an intelligent interest in pictures, and often in the lunch-hour I would run along to the National Gallery and study just one masterpiece. Francis Perrot was a brilliant reporter. He would go out on a job and then dictate his article to me. He usually contributed two or three paragraphs to the London Letter. He would say: 'I am going to milk my cows.' Which meant that

there were several people he could get on the 'phone
who would give him a bit of news—Frank Harris of
the Aborigines Protection Society, someone interested
in Proportional Representation, a contact in Bucking-
ham Palace, and so on. Dore would telephone his
report straight from the House of Commons. I would
take it down on the typewriter, using headphones, and
it would go in page by page to the Editor, who passed
it on to the telegraphists who put it in our private wire
to Manchester. The Manchester office had the whole
report five minutes after I had received it.

When war broke out in August 1914 I got the sack
on the very first day, together with the other small fry.
But I went on with my job as it was better than doing
nothing. I suppose the management thought that they
were in for a poor time financially, but as a matter of
fact, I think the next four years were the most prosperous in the life of the paper. The slogan 'Business
as Usual' was driven home to the advertisers, and the
Manchester Guardian published some very large supple-
ments. At that time England was very friendly with
China and the paper produced a great Chinese supple-
ment. It was rather fun going to the Chinese Embassy
in Portland Place with copy for the perusal of Mr Hi
or Mr Lo. The door was opened by a most imposing
English butler, and while I was waiting I was shown
in to a most beautiful room furnished with exquisite

Chinese pieces. I was particularly struck by the cabinets.

I was still living with my father and stepmother so that I could at least have breakfast. If I were home late, as I nearly always was, there was no supper for me. But my stepmother's maid, who had a heart of gold and who was sorry for me, would whisper to me in a conspiratorial voice that there was a packet of sandwiches for me behind such and such a book in my bedroom. Whenever I had time I had a meagre luncheon with Father in Aldersgate Street at an ABC shop.

Soon after war broke out, Mr G. H. Mair left the *Manchester Guardian* to work at the Foreign Office, and he offered me 30s. a week to go with him. I worked there for a very short time and I was utterly miserable. I had to type for Russian translators, and their English sounded like Russian and their writing was like nothing on earth. I had no friend, I saw nothing of Mr Mair who had engaged me, and when the *Manchester Guardian* wrote to me to say that they would be glad if I could go back there for the handsome salary of 35s. a week, I was overjoyed. I felt that I could now live on my own. I got a room in Golders Green for 10s. a week, and whenever the weather was not too bad I walked the six miles to the office, through Hampstead and St John's Wood, past the Zoological

Gardens, through Regent's Park where squirrels with ice-cold feet would jump on my hands and shoulders for sweet grapes, 2d. a quarter of a pound, up Portland Place to Regent Street, and on to Fleet Street. I thought it very romantic to walk part of the way to the office to the sound of the screaming of monkeys and the roaring of lions when I skirted the Zoo, and that way I saved sixpence, which I spent on breakfast at the Express Dairy: roll and butter, 2d., Cambridge sausage, 2d., and coffee, 2d. Whenever I could I scrounged lunch with Father. I was back with the work and the men that I loved, and I stayed with the *Manchester Guardian* until I met my husband at the end of the war.

I was overjoyed when Mr Bone gave me one or two reporting assignments, such as a London Letter paragraph about an economy exhibition which was being held in the new London County Council building on the banks of the Thames. We had nothing much in the way of air raids, except a few bombs dropped by Zeppelins at night, and we felt no apprehension when walking about the City in the lunch-hour. Sometimes I would go to fine organ recitals given in London churches for office workers by Walford Davies or Harold Darke.

Nearly every Friday evening Milly and I would go to the theatre, either to the pit, for which we queued and paid 2s. 6d., or on grand occasions to the dress circle or stalls with tickets given to me by Mr Bone. There was always in those days something good and cheering to see—fine Shakespeare productions at His Majesty's, drawing-room plays with Irene Vanbrugh or Gerald du Maurier, musical comedies with Gabrielle Ray, Gertie Millar, Phyllis and Zena Dare, and many others.

Once Mr Bone went to the Admiralty and left his umbrella there. He sent me to retrieve it, and who should hand it to me, beautifully packed up and sealed with an official Navy seal, but Mr Jack Gilliland, brother of my headmistress at the Haberdashers', and the spit and image of her. I had seen him on Sports Days and recognized him at once, but I was too shy to tell him that I was an old Haberdasher.

One Saturday morning we had a really nasty air-raid. We heard a lot of bangs, went to the office door, and the sky seemed to be full of Taubes. There was no opposition, as I believe our small air force was escorting the King and Queen on some official occasion. The Taubes seemed to be dropping their bombs on the City proper, beyond St Paul's Cathedral. I felt very anxious about Father, and when the All Clear was sounded Mr Perrot went with me to see how he had got on. We had to go by a roundabout way because the Post Office at Mount Pleasant was on fire and

Smithfield was a mass of débris and firemen's hoses. I was devoutly thankful to see Father and everyone in his warehouse all present and correct, but the place was a mass of powdered glass which was being swept up, and the factory or warehouse next door was eliminated, reduced to a heap of rubble. A clergyman was there praying with a small group of survivors. I think Father was as pleased to see me as I was to see him. When I got back to the office, Mr Bone asked me to write about what I had seen. I thought it a great honour to be asked to write anything, however trivial, for the paper.

Every third week-end I had from Friday evening until Monday morning free, and I generally went with Milly to the glorious little hamlet called Friday Street in Surrey, a district of pine forests, running streamlets and a lake, a Switzerland in miniature. Some of the cottages had ever-flowing ice-cold water piped to their back doors in wooden runnels. It was an ideal spot for a rest and change from the bustle of Fleet Street. We stayed with a dear elderly lady called Mrs Dixon, who had a tiny general store on the lake there. She charged us very little for the week-end. We had to get to the shop by crossing a plank over the water. The last time I went there, a few years ago, the shop had vanished, but the village was much the same, except that there was a pub which I did not remember. It was a glorious

centre for walks, up a foxglove-lined walk to the top
of Leith Hill, through the woods to Holmbury St
Mary, up Hindhead from which one had a view all
over Surrey. We used to bathe in the lake early in the
morning, until later on in the war when it was used
by German prisoners-of-war. They seemed to be
having a jolly good time and I should not think they
ever wished to escape. On Monday morning we used
to walk to Gomshall to catch a train which got us back
to the office in good time. The country there is gloriously unchanged and gloriously free from crowds,
except at week-ends when the motorists come out in
swarms.

After the Armistice on November 11th, 1918, I
worked solely for the editorial side, and had the
wonderful salary of £4 a week, so that I was able to
put 10s. in the Post Office Savings Bank. I was be-
coming quite a capitalist!

I was now twenty-eight years old and quite recon-
ciled to being a bachelor all my life. I loved my work
and saw no sign of a change. But my Guardian Angel
decreed otherwise. In the autumn of 1919, Howard
Spring, who had been demobilized from the army and
was working in the Reporters' Room of the *Manchester
Guardian* in Manchester, came to London to take the
place of a member of the staff who was away ill. We